STEP
BY STEP
INNOVATION

We Need It Now

John Gabrick

First Printing 2013

Printed in the United States of America

ISBN 978-0-578-12167-3

To Jan, Tara and Johnny

Contents

Introduction

I started early as an inventor, working as a lab rat with robotics and artificial intelligence in academia. I learned how to work the system in academia, and was fortunate enough to be able to take technology from the lab and commercialize it. Unfortunately, we met with only limited success. We mastered the intellectual property, research, design, and technology aspects, but completely neglected the business and marketing. After my stint in academia, I decided that I actually wanted to be paid for working, and went to graduate school to get an MBA to learn how to deal with the business side of commercialization. Either through a gift or a genetic defect, I've been an inventor, and have always pushed to have new ideas and methods implemented. Along the way, I learned a lot about the internal processes and roadblocks within an organization that do everything possible to discourage success. Sometimes I succeeded and sometimes I didn't. However, in every situation I learned more. I have been everything from inventor, to VP of engineering, to CEO, and have seen innovation from many different angles. I was also fortunate, or unfortunate, depending on how you look at it, to have a very rich education in intellectual property, getting a once-in-a-lifetime opportunity to be embroiled in a no-holds-barred legal battle. It was a full time skirmish for almost two years, and it provided an unbelievable experience into the world of intellectual property that I will never forget.

Soon afterward, I started helping companies with their innovation process, and have been doing this for more than a decade. I've interviewed thousands of people in hundreds of industries, academia, and legal organizations. I've heard every excuse and seen every tactic for spurring innovation. I was struck by the fact that innovation was so simple, yet so complex. It was something that everyone had a theory for, yet few people continuously succeeded at. I wanted to make it better. This book is a story taken from these experiences. I wanted to try to show people that their situation is probably not that different from others who are trying to run an innovation program as well as present tactics for ensuring that they're successful. Of course, there are lots of scenarios and possible outcomes, but if you can follow the basic steps outlined in this book, you'll have a much better than average chance of success.

Good luck!

Why You Should Read This Book

As an innovation experiment, one of the most respected and innovative companies in the world embarked on a six week journey to find innovative new products within their organization. It wasn't that they weren't already coming up with new products; they just wanted more, as innovative companies always seem to do. They used the same techniques that are discussed in this book, and within that short time frame (and with a very small group of people: less than 500) uncovered a new product that had been dormant in the organization for years. In short order they commercialized it, and it went on to generate nearly $40 million in new revenue. This was just an experiment.

In another example, a $6 billion financial institution used this methodology to uncover service improvements within their organization. Because they were a cost center, they were constantly under pressure to come up with ways to lower costs and improve efficiency. They ran a small experiment with about 100 people and uncovered a treasure trove of ideas. Their question to those initial employees was "How can we save $5/day?" The answers were so overwhelmingly successful that they created an entire new group dedicated to soliciting employee ideas and implementing them.

Finally, in an impressive feat of how quickly this can work, a small group (about 250) of IT professionals were challenged with ways to improve their operating processes by the vice president of the division. He gave his group 24 hours to come up with ideas, and personally monitored the progress over the course of the day. The success was rapid, with over 60% participation and nearly 85 ideas in just the first few hours. The success spread so quickly, that another department joined in. Not to be outdone, this second vice president also entered a challenge and solicited ideas from her division. The competition between the two departments drove participation to nearly 100% and produced nearly 50 actionable projects.

Characters

John Jones, *Manager of the Technical Products Division*

Cindy Vinatoni, *VP of Engineering*

Mr. Poprek, *John Jones' former boss*

Bill Smith, *CEO*

Frank Caliente, *IP Counsel*

Jay Boroke, *Engineer*

Janice Koerth, *Engineer*

Sam English, *Engineer*

Mike Orlowski, *HR Director*

Napolean Taseme, *IT Director*

Amelda, *software programmer for the prior innovation system*

Nicola Wayne, *communications director*

Tony Hernandez, *VP of Marketing*

Katie Croslinski, *Physician Coordinator*

Chris Highbrooke, *New Business Development*

Bernie Pralene, *VP of Sales at Twinevil Corp*

The Loss

" . . . and further, all travel and non-essential expenses will be immediately cut. As managers, you'll be expected to cut anywhere from 15 to
30% from your operating budget, and we're going to immediately review
all budgets for opportunities to make further reductions. We're in a tough
position, but we can beat this. We have good people and good products,
and if we can just get our costs back in line we'll have more ammunition to
fight Twinevil Corp. As we maneuver through this, I'll communicate with
you further about the details of our strategy.

"I have great confidence in our company and will guarantee that I'll
fight for us until we have come out of this. Thank you for your time." Bill
Smith, CEO of Medacmet Industries had finished his all-hands message to
the managers, announcing that Twinevil Corp had just formally registered
their purchase of a five percent stake in Medacmet Industries.

"*This is unbelievable*," thought John Jones, Manager of the Technical
Products division of Medacmet Industries.

John Jones had only been with Medacmet Industries for three months
and was just getting up to speed. The fact is he actually wasn't surprised.
While Medacmet Industries was a household name, their revenues had
been flat for the last 7 quarters, and earnings had practically disappeared

except for the "creative accounting" that the finance department had been playing with international currency, tax laws and haphazard mergers and acquisitions.

Part of what the CEO had said was true; they had a good group of people and fairly decent products. The problem was that most of their products had been around for years, and the profit margins had fallen as they continued to make cost-cutting changes. You know, improving the manufacturing process to save 2%, change to plastics to save another 1%, and so on, all in an effort to squeeze the last remaining margins out of the same products. The problem was that their market share also continued to shrink, so those cost reductions had simply offset the loss of customers. They had made a few attempts at launching new products, but they had been met with limited success. One new product in particular had looked extremely promising. It received great customer reviews, was well supported by upper management, and had been a manufacturing godsend. Unfortunately, they had been blind sided by Twinevil Corp's similar product, and the worst part was that Twinevil Corp had also launched a lawsuit claiming patent infringement. While they tried to fight the lawsuit, it was clear that they didn't have the necessary records to verify their development; but even if they did, Twinevil Corp had come up with the concept far earlier and would have beat them anyway.

John Jones sat at this desk and pondered the situation. He had incidentally received a job offer from Twinevil Corp, and could probably get a position with them if he wanted to. The tough part was that John actually believed that Medacmet Industries was a better company, had better technologies, and could actually beat Twinevil Corp in the marketplace. After all, when he accepted the job with Medacmet Industries that was part of his charter. Now, he simply had less time to make it happen.

John knew that revenue and earnings growth had been poor, and that the primary cause had been lack of innovation. He also knew that continuing to cut costs was the opposite of what they should be doing. His first stop would be to talk with Bill Smith, the CEO.

How Long Does it Take to Count to Infinity?

I've had my fair share of meetings attempting to convince executive management of the need for innovation. At a visceral level, everyone agrees that innovation is critical to success, but when it comes down to pulling the trigger, there seems to be apprehension. I can remember sitting in a meeting with the VP of R&D at a billion dollar conglomerate talking about innovation. He stated emphatically that innovation was simply "their job" and there should be no need for systems, reviews, and rewards. His argument was that his team was comprised of highly-skilled (majority were PhDs), well-paid employees who didn't need anything extra in order to innovate. To some degree he was right—these people were innovating on a daily basis. There were several problems, though. First, they weren't innovating toward any specific goals. Researchers had general areas of investigation, but were rarely provided with a specific problem to work on. Second, this existing research was full time, and deviations outside of their specific areas were unknowingly discouraged because they were not allowed the time to make these unexplained forays. Third, there was no reward (other than keeping their job) for coming up with new innovations. Let's face it, innovation is a personally-driven process, and there is no way to measure whether someone is "innovating" on a daily basis. In other words, I'm not going to get into trouble for not innovating, and in some organizations, I'll get in more trouble if I do. Which reminds me of another story.

I was sitting in a meeting with a VP of Marketing trying to convince him that he should try innovation...again. During our conversation, he pulled a massive three-ring binder from a shelf behind his desk, and dropped it in front of me. It hit with a thud. This, he said, was our innovation process. He explained how they had paid a major consulting firm nearly seven figures (ouch!) to come up with an innovation program tailored to their exact needs. They spent months interviewing employees, looking at the market, and building a customized solution. He further explained that they launched the program with what seemed like great success and received thousands of ideas as a result. They picked a few and implemented them with fairly good success, but when they tried to replicate the success they failed. To make a long story short, they violated one of the main tenants of successful innovation—they didn't comment or respond to any of the participants in the program that didn't have the best ideas. In fact, they never communicated the results to any of the participants, virtually guaranteeing future failure.

Why is this story important? Because most organizations are not trying innovation for the first time. Many are making their second, third, fourth, or higher attempt. The 'why' is obvious; innovation is critical to organization success. The real question is, "why did they fail so many times in the past?" There are a couple of reasons. First, many times there is no 'organizational memory', meaning that no one really remembers any of the details of prior efforts, or they have a misguided reason why it failed. Second, and more likely, is that they keep leaving out a key ingredient. Take the example of baking a cake. Here are the typical ingredients for making a simple white cake:

> *sugar*
> *butter*
> *eggs*
> *vanilla extract*
> *all-purpose flour*
> *baking powder*
> *milk*

Most people could do a good job of assembling the ingredients, but if asked how much of each, in what order, and with what technique they should be used to create a cake, most would fail. In many cases, a single missing ingredient or incorrect amount will yield a mess. Innovation is no different. On the surface, it seems quite simple, but if the ingredients are not combined in the proper way, you'll fail—repeatedly.

The Plan

"Good afternoon, Bill. I heard your message earlier today, and I just want you to know that I'm prepared to do whatever it takes to save Medacmet Industries. Bill, when you hired me three months ago, I told you that I would be undertaking an aggressive campaign to breathe life into our organization's innovation processes."

"Yes, I remember."

"Well, Bill, while watching our costs is a good idea, we absolutely must invest in our innovation process as well."

"John, this is war. This is not a friendly merger, they want to dismantle Medacmet Industries. We have enough of a war chest to counter them. Our stock price is at an all-time low; we're extremely vulnerable."

"Bill, what if I could help raise our stock price and simultaneously grow our revenues and earnings?"

"I'm all ears."

"Innovation is the key to this," said John. "Let's face it, we haven't had a truly original product in over six years. We've become super-efficient at managing costs, but we're practically incapable of managing our 'revenue generation' capabilities."

"Not true, John. Our revenues have been growing at a constant 4.5%

over the past several years."

"Yes, but how? With acquisitions? Those were just empty attempts to build the revenue. They brought no real value to the organization. Even our analysts lambasted us for those acquisitions, and it's not surprising, as eighty percent of all acquisitions fail. The only bright spot was the acquisition of Syntactical Labs, and most of the people here don't know much about what they could do for us."

"OK, smart guy, maybe you're right, but we just don't have the time to build innovation into our current organization. I'd love to sit on a beanbag chair and brainstorm about the future, but we're a bit beyond that. I need results yesterday."

"Give me just a few weeks to get started. You're right, it doesn't happen overnight, but we'll have a short-term plan to get some immediate results, and a long-term plan to really build the capabilities. We'll be able to publicize the short-term results and influence the financial markets about our prospects for the future."

"I don't know. I've been encouraging our employees to be more innovative for years, and all I have to show for it is a few more patents, and higher legal bills."

"Bill, that's a very typical outcome. The CEOs of every company have been saying the same thing as well. If my hunch is right, I would bet that our employees really don't know what it means to be innovative."

"What do you mean?"

"Innovation is something different to almost everyone. Some people think it's turning off their computers at night to save money, while others think you want business plans for markets we wouldn't even consider. And, you're not too far off when you talk about beanbag chairs and whiteboards either. Many still believe that innovation is this mystical process that defies definition. But the real answer is that innovation can be built into a process, and research has shown that the organizations that have an innovation process far outpace their competitors that don't. To get short-term results, we have to focus people's effort on the goals that mean the most to the company."

"Give me an example."

"Well, let's take cost-cutting as an example. You've told everyone that they have to cut costs by 15-20%. Most will just fire or layoff people and cut travel to meet the goals."

"So?"

"With all due respect, it's short-sighted. They end up getting rid of people they need, stopping research projects, and effectively eliminating our chances to actually grow and create. The problem is you don't find out about it until it's too late. Let's try something different."

"I know that we have higher manufacturing costs in the Milwaukee plant than Twinevil Corp does. From the people I've talked with, we probably waste at least 15% of our production cost in missed production and errors."

"I'm well aware of that. We've had a dozen consultants look at that process. Nobody has come up with anything. The last group of consultants charged us six figures to come up with a new process, but didn't consider the costs of implementing it. It did save us a few percent, but it cost a fortune."

"Let's try asking the machine operators what they think."

"Been there. Done that."

"And, what happened?"

"We got a few good ideas, but most of it was junk. The other problem was we had a big influx, and then it just died off within a few weeks. Suddenly no one had any more ideas."

"Did you implement any of the ideas?"

"One of two, but nothing was good enough."

"Did you reward the people who provided the good ideas?"

"Are you kidding? We pay those guys good money to run those machines. They should be giving us improvements as part of their job. They're saving their own jobs. Besides, most of the ideas came from the shop foreman."

"I see. What about the review of the ideas? Who did it?"

"The shop foreman and some people that he selected."

"I see. Did they follow some set of criteria to review the ideas?"

"I don't know. I figure the shop foreman should be a pretty good judge regarding improvements. He has been there 20 years, and really knows his stuff."

"You mean he has been there 20 years and they still have a waste problem?"

"Well, yes, but he is doing a good job."

"I'm not saying that he isn't talented, but maybe he is a bit prejudiced. It's not an uncommon problem. Recent research studies have established that 70% or more of new ideas come from the people who actually do the work. So, by the law of averages, you should have seen quite a few good ideas from the shop floor workers."

"70%!?"

"Yes. In February 2000, Southwest Airline CEO Herb Kelleher sent a letter concerning the current fuel cost crisis to the home of every employee. An excerpt read, "Jet fuel costs three times what it did one year ago. Southwest uses 19 million gallons a week. Our profitability is in jeopardy." He asked each worker to help by saving $5.00 a day. The response was immediate, and within six weeks of the letter being sent to the employees, this large organization found ways to save more than $2 million dollars."

"Wow."

"Here's another. During WWII, a junior officer in the South China Sea suggested modifications to gun turrets that were repeatedly rejected by superiors. He persisted for years and eventually the changes were recognized and implemented. It took a long time to recognize his contribution because no one believed that an idea of this magnitude could come from someone so junior in the organization. The modifications ended up yielding a 3000% increase in performance, and are credited with helping the U.S. Navy win the war."

"The point is, Bill, that there are probably lots more like this in our own company. The problem is that innovation is not a part-time job for a disinterested subcommittee."

"We have a dedicated person who works on ideas."

"Who?"

"Sam English."

"Sam! Everyone thinks he's crazy."

"He is, but he is very smart."

"I'm sure he is, but he clearly doesn't have the kind of skills to run an innovation process. Tell me, would you trust a single person to run your accounting department?"

"No. It's far too important."

"Exactly. So, why trust one person to run innovation? Accounting is a cost center. Innovation is a profit center. Sam is excellent at helping to analyze "fringe" concepts, but there is more required in an innovation process."

"OK, tell me what the pieces are."

"Alright, let's start at the top. Strong management support is the first requirement. The company must know that you're committed to innovation." John emphasized by pointing directly at Bill, "Since innovation will be an enterprise endeavor, we're bound to encounter those who will resist. That is why it will be important for you to provide influence and demonstrate the value at a company-wide level."

"That sounds easy enough."

"Basically, it is. The words will be easy, but you'll be required to spend some of your time on it as well. You might be needed to review high-level ideas or provide feedback and support to participants. It will be important that you show everyone that you're rolling up your sleeves and actively participate. The impact will be huge if you make comments on various ideas; after all, everyone is looking to impress the boss."

"Don't put too much weight on my opinion, I'm easy to impress," joked Bill. "What's next?"

"The establishment of strategic challenges or focus areas."

"That was a mouthful, you want to explain that?" questioned Bill.

"Sure, we need to give the participants in our innovation program some goals. We'll get much more meaningful results if we ask employees for solutions to problems that are germane to us. Just like the CEO of Southwest Airlines did."

"So, like asking the shop floor employee about improving the manufacturing process?"

"Yes, exactly. We need to determine what we want out of this process. Technology issues, competitors, customer needs, as well as high-cost areas need to be examined. It will be important to make sure that these focus areas are specific enough so that people will be able to understand and respond, and most importantly, review. If we try to be too broad, then we'll get lots of ideas, most of which will not be relevant, and then reviewing them will be tedious and unproductive."

John continued with more points to consider for the innovation process.

"We'll also have to make resources available for all of this, particularly the review and implementation phases. We'll try to make sure we have high-quality responses with a good innovation challenge, but we'll have to spend quality time reviewing each of these ideas according to our predetermined criteria. It will be important to perform a thorough analysis of each idea for two reasons. First, we want to find the best ideas to implement, and second, we want to make sure that all of the people who spent the time responding to our challenge are provided feedback on why or why not their idea was chosen. And then, once ideas are selected, we'll need resources to implement them. While I can't promise that they'll all be easy to implement, there will be a high number of the selected idea-submitters who will want to participate in the implementation, and they typically will do the job faster and more effectively."

"We will also have to build a communications plan. It doesn't have to be fancy—it just has to communicate the facts—and it should really come from you, Bill, or one of your executive reports. While in other situations I've seen fancy video presentations and marketing materials, they're not necessary. Email is so ubiquitous that a well-crafted message will be sufficient to get started."

"Part of the communications will also have to address what we'll do with 'good' and 'bad' ideas. We'll want to make sure that we let everyone knows how their idea will be reviewed and implemented. We need to make the process 'see-through.' This establishes credibility for the process, and will encourage participation not only now, but also in the future."

"How are we going to keep track of all of this?"

"Well, the last part will be to map our process into a software tool that can keep track of all of the ideas, reviews, comments, and people."

"Not more software. We're still trying to swallow the bitter pill from the implementation of our ERP system. I don't think anyone has the stomach for another one."

"Don't worry, I've done this before. The implementation of this type of system is fast and painless. Remember, most people will only be doing basic tasks such as entering ideas and making comments. However, our reviewers and managers will need more tools to manage the entire flow of ideas. It's too much to try and manage with a spreadsheet. And, an additional benefit of this type of system is the ability to manage our intellectual property more effectively."

"John, this sounds like a lot of work."

"It is, Bill, but if we do it right, most of the time we spend will be on ideas that we believe we'll be implementing. Part of the success will be including your executive team and finding out what their issues are in order to develop strong innovation challenges. People work a little harder and smarter when they are working on their own problems. Think about it. If I told you that I'm going to help you solve one of your most pressing business issues, do you think you'd be interested?"

"Yes, but probably a little skeptical too."

"Fair enough. Let me have the job of convincing them. The nice part about this is that success breeds success, and if we follow these steps, we'll have a steady stream of people lining up not only to give us potential business challenges, but also to provide the resources we need to help them. Did you ever hear the story of Nail Soup?"

Innovation Best Practices

1. Focused business challenges
2. Make resources available
3. Establish and communicate budgets
4. Decide what happens to good ideas
5. Encourage participation
6. Feedback essential to build respect for the process
7. Guarantee cycle times and reviews

"Yes, you mean where the poor relative visits the rich relative and promises to make soup with just a nail?"

"Yes, that's the one."

"I see what you're saying. In the story, the poor relative ends up creating soup with just a nail, but with the help of the rich relative's carrots, potatoes, and other vegetables."

"Yes, the secret is that the rich relative provides the resources, or in this case, the vegetables, a little bit at a time, as he sees progress. The story ends with the rich relative asking the other to come back and make more soup. If we do this right, your team will be begging us to come back and make more Nail Soup."

"Okay, John, I'm convinced. I'll give you my support and I'll let my executive team know what's coming, and I'll tell them that they'll only need a nail!"

The Psychological Contract

I was sitting with the CEO of a medical products company discussing his need for innovation. He was fully supportive of the need, but questioned whether his own people could, "come up with something good." He stated that he was always happy to look at new ideas, but that there was, "never enough thought put into them." When I asked him how much thought he expected from an idea, he reached into his desk and pulled out a 10+ page document. He quickly flipped through the pages and rattled off typical business plan sections, such as marketing, competitor analysis, financial calculations, and manufacturability. I laughed when he first showed me, but quickly realized that he was absolutely serious. His argument for the detail was that he couldn't judge the viability of an idea without this information.

"Good point, but you're asking way too much from your people," I countered. I told him, "If you expected that for every idea that I submitted, I can tell you there is no way you'd get anything from me." He was puzzled. I explained that there is a psychological contract between the employee and the employer. You start with a small contribution (the idea), and then slowly build the value by looking at the details in an incremental fashion. If you were looking to build a new house, you'd start with design sketches, or even just a conversation about what you wanted. It wouldn't make any sense to provide you with complete engineering drawings before I even showed you a picture of it, would it?

He agreed.

Building Consensus

John could hardly wait to get started. He had arguably gotten the hardest part: the commitment from the CEO. He'd be able to use his authority to get the meetings he needed and to begin to develop the business challenges. There was still a lot to do, and John knew that he had to get his ducks in a row before he met with Cindy Vinatoni, the VP of Engineering, about potential challenges. Cindy was smart, but she had a no-nonsense approach and would quickly find the weaknesses in his plan. John decided to go after a business challenge that was more engineering-related simply because Medacmet Industries was heavy with technical resources, and a business challenge in this area would be easier to construct and market. While other areas of the business would certainly yield larger ROIs, the logic was harder to prove. For example, if he went to marketing and they ended up selecting an idea that created a whole new market, it could be worth hundreds of millions of dollars, but it would be a hard sell, at least for now. John knew that lots of innovation programs had failed because the expectations were set too high. He recalled a meeting with a boss at his previous employer.

"John, this innovation program isn't working. I only have two half-way decent proposals on my desk from the last six months. I thought you said you could drive innovation?"

"Mr. Poprek, I did say I could drive innovation, but you've put up too many obstacles."

"What do you mean? Everyone here is supposed to innovate, it's part of their job. All you had to do was get it out of them."

"I understand, but innovation is a little more sensitive than that."

"What do you mean?"

"Well, providing you with good ideas is not really in anyone's job description."

"That's ridiculous! Every person at this company has a yearly goal of providing four suggestions."

"Yes, but you've created a process that punishes creativity and dissuades anyone from giving you anything but 'suggestion box' type ideas."

"Ridiculous! Do you remember the Washing Piston idea that Dave Sabatical invented several years ago? He was awarded $25,000 in cash!"

"Yes, I remember. He worked on the idea for years, mostly outside of work. His concept was repeatedly rejected, and he was told several times that he was only to work on billable jobs. I honestly don't know why he endured so much, but I do remember that he left the company about a year later. I think he started his own company?"

"He wasn't qualified to take his idea to the next step. He had no management experience."

"Maybe so, but I think his company just closed a $5 million round of venture capital funding."

"That's beside the point, John. People quit all of the time. You were hired to build innovation, and I don't see it working. How come I don't have any more of these?" as he pointed to the two forty-plus page documents on his desk.

"I don't mean to be disrespectful, sir, but nobody is going to spend their own time writing up a 40 page document with complete production, marketing, sales, and financial information on the slight chance that it will be accepted by you."

"Ridiculous. I went through each of these very carefully. They just don't merit additional funding or effort. Besides, how am I supposed to decide if we have a viable idea if I only have a paragraph to read? Business decisions require detailed information in a plethora of areas."

"I understand, Mr. Poprek, but some of your executive team thought the ideas were pretty good."

"Ridiculous. I've seen these ideas before and they haven't. They'll never work."

"Well, sir, once again, no disrespect, but I think you've clearly outlined why we don't have any other ideas. We require people to spend hundreds of hours researching every possible contingency, write it up in a 40 page document, talk with the superiors, build consensus, and then leave it up to one person to make the decision. "

"What are trying to say, John?"

"I think you've helped me to reach a personal decision about working here."

In retrospect, John may have acted in haste, but the decision was inevitable. In this situation, the organization was unwilling to change, particularly at the top. Innovation was given plenty of lip service, but the environment was just not conducive to success. While consensus decision-making is not a requirement of a successful innovation management program, open-mindedness is.

As he began his job of building consensus, he would be on the lookout for the idea killers.

His meeting with Cindy was in the morning. He'd be prepared.

VP Engineering

"Good morning, Cindy," said John. "I scheduled this meeting to talk with you about our new innovation program."

"Good morning, John. Yes, I know. Bill sent me an email and then caught me in the hallway about it. He said something about Nail Soup." She laughed for a minute and then got right down to business.

"Bill told me that you've got some new ideas about how innovation ought to work around here. I'm all for innovating, but remember, Bill is sitting in his ivory tower over in the corner office. He doesn't have to get product out the door like I do. I don't have to tell you that we're all busy around here. And after his announcement, I have even more work. We were already low on resources and now he is asking for more cuts. I have no choice, but I'm going to have to let people go, John. Good people. I admire your determination, but I think maybe you've picked the wrong time to try something like this."

John sat forward in his chair. He knew that this was going to be difficult, but she had a couple of good points, particularly about laying off people. People don't feel too innovative when they are worried about their job. Nonetheless, he started.

"Cindy, you make some good points. As I mentioned to Bill, I don't expect this to be an easy process, but I do expect good results. In fact, now, more than ever, we are in desperate need of innovation. Research study after research study has shown that innovation is the key to both profitability and competitive success. New, innovative products have higher profit margins, help capture new markets and customers, and can make formidable intellectual property obstacles."

"John, that's all well and good, but it's not easy to just come up with a new, innovative product. It takes years of research, lots of resources, and a bit of luck. Unfortunately, we're not in a position to come up with any of that. I have to worry about getting our next version shipped this quarter. If I don't make that happen, we lose money, lots of money, then we have even less resources and we'll all be looking for new jobs shortly thereafter."

"First, let me say that I agree with your analysis, partly. New product development can be time-consuming and expensive; however, you're overlooking the luck, or rather, the innovative aspect. Who's to say the next revolutionary product will be expensive or time-consuming? Some of the best innovations are simply a different combination of off-the-shelf components. I like to call it the 'chocolate and peanut butter' idea."

"Cute, John, but I'm cutting back on sweets," she said slyly.

"Let me tell you a story that might entice you to try some fat-free chocolate."

"I like chocolate, so go ahead."

"In a previous situation, I worked with a company that was in the paint business. They organized their business according to markets, so they had a division for residential paint, appliance paint, automotive paint, aircraft paint, and road paint. The divisions were all located in different areas, and they did very little collaboration. One day as I was talking with the general manager of the automotive business, she lamented that their market was stagnant and they had seen little growth in the last few years. She expressed how she'd like to uncover some 'breakthrough products' and had tasked her R&D group with coming up with new ideas. In particular, she talked about producing automobile paint that would be scratch-proof as many of their customers talked about the value that could be added not only to the consumer's vehicle, but also to the price increase that would be possible. Alas, the problem had eluded them, and a solution seemed far away. As she told me this story, I laughed, at which point she asked me what I found to be so funny. I told her that during a similar meeting with the appliance paint division, they had told me about a product they developed several years ago—scratch-proof paint—the exact thing she was looking for. I also told her that the appliance group had shelved it almost immediately as there was little demand or value-add for appliances that were scratch-proof. What customer would pay a premium so that they wouldn't scratch their washing machine? None. Well, the rest of the story is history. The formulation for scratch-proof paint was shared with the automotive division and it was an instant success, increasing revenues by 25% the first year it was introduced, and even better results in later years. The cost was near zero and the product was introduced to the market almost immediately."

"Sounds too good to be true."

"I know it does, but it's true. The nice thing is that this same type of innovation is probably locked up in our own organization."

"Maybe I should reconsider cutting back on sweets…"

"Perhaps. However, innovation can also be about reducing waste or going after new markets with our existing products. Plus, we're not going to tackle that problem right now. Since we're just starting our innovation initiative, we are going to bite off a small piece by going after a manageable issue within Product Engineering. I know for a fact that our KD1999 product is deficient in a number of areas, and more specifically, that our competitors are eating our lunch in the market with their products."

"Nice try, but we've been looking at this same problem for the last six months as well. We've got a couple of good ideas on the drawing board, and should probably have something by the end of this year. And it wasn't an easy fix. It's probably going to cost us close to $5 million to make this adjustment."

"Who came up with the idea?"

"Sam English. That guy is a genius," she said.

"How did he come up with his solution?"

"Not sure, he just came to me one day with his idea on a piece of drafting paper. We ran it by manufacturing, and they said that it wouldn't be a problem. Sam even applied for a patent, and legal thinks we have a good shot at getting it."

"OK, we'll do it."

"Do what?"

"That will be our challenge."

"Challenge for what?"

"As part of the innovation program, we're going to address an issue that is currently causing us lots of pain, and see if we can come up with a better solution."

"John, once again, I admire your determination, but let's move on. This problem has been solved."

"For $5 million?" he asked quizzically.

"You do what ya gotta do."

"What if we could find a solution that costs half of that amount? What if it costs only 10%? What if it could be implemented in two months?"

"If you could find a solution that saved us just 50% and could be implemented in six months, I'd ask you what you were smoking."

"I'll tell you what, we'll come up with two challenges. This will be the first challenge, and as backup, we'll come up with another one. How's that?"

"Okay, but we have two issues to deal with."

"What are they?"

"They are both named Sam English. I don't think he's going to be too happy about trying to come up with a different design. He's put a lot of work into his design."

"Fair enough. Let me talk with him. If I can convince him to give it a try, will you support the initiative?"

"Sure."

"Cindy, I'm serious. If this is going to work, I want the message to come from you stating that this is important. And I'm going to want you and a few other members of the engineering team to review all of the possible ideas."

"Me?!"

"Yes, you, and a few members of the engineering department. If people know that you are looking at the ideas, we're going to get much better participation, and much better ideas. And I'm going to need a few other things from you as well," he continued.

"I'm going to need you to sponsor a few rewards, and agree to recognize the people who come up with the winning idea."

"That's a big IF. If they can come up with an idea."

"No problem."

"John, I can't help to notice, but you've got me pretty committed here. You want me to make an announcement, give you some of my engineers to do reviews, have me spend my valuable time looking at ideas, and then dig into my budget for rewards. This is a tall order."

"Cindy, look, I will need your engineers to go through and review each idea, but we'll use an automated process for that. It will still take time, but only a couple of days at the most. It's going to be important that they look at every idea, review it, and make comments. Think about it from the idea-submitter's perspective. If they spend time thinking about the issues and then responding, we owe them the courtesy of a reply. Everyone who participates will be interested in the outcomes. It's just human nature. And, if we don't, you'll be ruining your chances to do this again."

"You mean if I want to do this again."

"Right, if you want to. We're just going to make sure that it works the right way. Besides, it will be a good chance for some of the newer employees to be recognized by their more experienced peers."

"Okay, but I don't have time to go through all the ideas—pardon the expression—that may be 'junk,' after this is finished."

"Understand. It won't be junk. You won't have to be part of every review, only when they are reviewing the final entries, just a few hours. Everyone wants to impress the boss, so your participation will be critical. Besides, you probably won't find too much junk. We're going to eliminate a lot of that by making sure that the challenge is well crafted. Also, remember that the submitter's name will be on the idea and everyone will have a chance to see it. Peer feedback will keep a lot of that in check."

"That sounds alright, but what about the rewards. I told you we don't have any budget. Remember, we're trying to cut our budget. I don't have

25 grand to give someone."

"I understand, but we don't need to have a huge paycheck, instead you'll have more success with something personal, like an MP3 player or camera. Surely you can 'find' enough money in your budget for a few hundred dollars."

"Probably."

"One of the biggest misconceptions is that people want money for their ideas. Most prefer a personal reward. In today's world, most money is direct-deposited into your checking account. If you were to award someone $1000, they'd probably never see it; it would go to pay the mortgage or the electric bill. But an MP3 player is something you can brag about. We'll post the winners on the bulletin board by the front-door and on the company intranet portal."

"I don't know, John. This sounds like a big project."

"It is, sort of. We'll spend a few more minutes here making sure that our challenge is put together correctly, I'll give you a short email to approve for the announcement, and you'll spend a few hours reviewing ideas. And just think, it this works, and we save a few million dollars, you're going to be a heroine."

"Cute, John, I'm already a superwoman in this job, but it might help avoid some cuts."

"Great."

"And just remember, you still have to convince Sam English."

"That's fine. I'll contact him today along with the reviewers from your department."

John and Cindy continued their meeting for a few more minutes and finalized the challenge along with the prizes. Cindy opted for an MP3 player and dinner for two at Jacksons. The final challenge was:

Ideas for increasing the speed by which the Kidney Dialysis, KD1999, can perform dialysis.

Before he talked with Sam, though, he wanted to talk with the company's Intellectual Property attorney, Frank Caliente.

A Matter of National Security

For many of these folks, innovation is a dream that they can only imagine. Most of their day is spent fighting fires, preparing for product releases, and answering to marketing. It's hard to think about sailing your boat to the Caribbean when it has a hole in it. So, why not ask them about the hole and help them fix it? As it turns out, this is very powerful.

Shortly after 9/11, the United States was hit with an anthrax scare. As it would turn out, I had previously scheduled a meeting with one of our customers in New York, and since innovation was critical, we decided not to postpone our meeting. We were having some trouble getting traction with innovation in her organization. As I met my contact at the front door, she turned to me and said, "I just got a call from the Department of Defense. They want to know if we can help them solve the problem of anthrax being sent through the U.S. mail." You may recall that not only was the U.S. dealing with the myriad of issues surrounding the World Trade Center, but also there was some unknown person(s) sending deadly anthrax spores through the U.S. mail. As you can imagine, this was a major problem. Since the spores were small, they could be sent in a regular letter. Because of this, there were millions of pieces of mail that could be hiding this deadly toxin, and because an unwitting victim only had to breathe in the powdery dust once to become infected, panic was widespread and real.

"I wish we could solve that one," she said, "they called us because we have one of the largest and diversified group of engineers and technical resources in the country. They figured that with all of this intellectual horsepower, we had to have some ideas floating around."

Since our Innovator system had already been installed, we already had a 'connection' to all of the people, skills, and knowledge. We just had to make a 180 degree turn. Instead of collecting ideas, we would advertise this problem to her entire engineering group. We could use the collective knowledge of her entire organization to solve the problem. We'd have engineers and technical experts from all disciplines creating and collaborating on trying to find a way to detect anthrax while it was still being sorted and in transit.

The response was absolutely overwhelming. We had a very focused problem (of which everyone could appreciate the severity), a group of highly talented and diverse engineers, a deadline, and significant rewards to the inventor (solving a major national issue), AND would make the boss happy. This was the boss's "hole in the boat." It was no surprise that the relevant solution was discovered within days.

IP Counsel

From prior experience, John knew that Frank Caliente would probably not be interested in rocking the boat. Frank had a process for dealing with inventions, and he was known for being thorough, but unwavering in how he did things. Frank was used to participating in monthly invention review meetings, and it was his decision about whether or not to move forward with inventions to the patenting process. He didn't much see the value of 'ideas,' likening them to being a waste of time. John realized that he'd probably not run into many objections from Frank, but his goal was to get him excited about the whole innovation concept. John knew that with strong intellectual property support, new ideas could become insurmountable competitive barriers.

"Hello, Frank"

"How are you doing, John. I understand that you are working on some new innovation initiative."

"Yes, sure am. I wanted to talk with you about how you could participate."

"I'm happy to help, but really, coming up with new innovation is for the engineers. I just do the legal work. And, lately that has included more and more of defending Medacmet Industries in patent infringement lawsuits."

"Well, what I'm working on will initially focus on the innovation side, but we'll be putting in place new processes that should greatly help us from a litigation perspective."

"No offense, John, but the legal realm is a little out of your area of responsibility."

"Frank, you're right. It is. However, consider the benefits if everyone in the organization understood the basic legal concepts and how that might help us to forward your legal strategy. For example, if the engineering department understood the basic concepts of a trade secret—that it can't even be disclosed in an off-hand manner—as well as the fact that trade secrets are the keystone of our competitive advantage, it could have a major impact. I don't know anyone that can even name any of our trade secrets, and considering how difficult it is to keep them secret; teaching people what they are and how to protect them would be tantamount. The major theme of our innovation program is the realization that ideas do become important intellectual property."

"I agree, we think of our IP strategy as successful if we prevent our competitors from copying our products, or at least make it more expensive for them to work around our IP. We need to build more IP. It's painful to see that Twinevil Corp has one of the most diverse patent portfolios, and consequently is one of the most profitable organizations."

"So, if we could turn more ideas into IP, then it might help us ward off litigation in the future. Didn't we just lose a lawsuit to Twinevil Corp because we couldn't prove when the inventor actually invented the solution?"

"That's a bit of an oversimplification, John. There are lots of reasons why we didn't win, and by the way, we're going to appeal that decision."

"I'm sure that we will, but wouldn't it be nice if you didn't have to worry about whether our invention documentation was accurate, or whether the engineers knew how to properly research and comment on potential inventions and ideas? Everyone knows that the idea Twinevil Corp litigated was really invented here, but that we had no documentation. Plus the fact that the main inventor went to Twinevil Corp didn't really help."

"This stuff is complex, John. As I said, there are lots of reasons why we lost—and as I mentioned, we are appealing—but the bottom line is that a couple of pieces of paper might have prevented a lot of this from happening."

"There is a lot of history at Medacmet Industries, Frank, 75 years of it. One of the benefits of the innovation program will be to catalog and document all of our new ideas as well as our historical ones, at least the ones where we can find documentation. Then, you'd be able to quickly search for and find similar ideas or inventions, and possibly create patent applications that cover technologies we've created everywhere in the organization, making sure that we don't duplicate effort and that we properly determine all of the inventors for a particular invention. You'll be able to tell exactly when an idea was first created, who created it, how it was modified, and who had access to it. Then, if that idea ever becomes patentable, you'll have a complete record from its inception. As a side benefit, since the information will be available electronically, the inventors will be able to participate more in the invention process, and won't need to bother you about the status of their inventions in the patenting process."

"I like that aspect, we spend an inordinate amount of time just answering routine questions, but I have a couple of concerns. First, if all of this information is available electronically, then that means it's also discoverable, meaning that in a lawsuit, we'd have to give them all of the information in our system. Second, I'm a bit reticent about having our company intellectual property stored electronically. There are a lot of hackers out there."

"Good points, Frank. Let me start with the first one, electronic discovery. First of all, you're right, this information could be discoverable in a lawsuit, but what's the difference between having the ideas and inventions reside on a thousand different PCs versus a central repository? We never back up computers when employees leave, so we can never find any information, case in point: our recent lawsuit with Twinevil Corp. If we had his backup information on the computer, you could argue that there might not ever have been a lawsuit. It would have been open and shut. Plus the inventor would have been liable for possible theft of intellectual property. We may have been getting triple damages for them stealing our intellectual property instead of trying to defend ourselves from a patent infringement suit."

John continued, "We could have further prevented loss, by simply letting this inventor know (when he left for Twinevil Corp) that we had the complete record on when his ideas were invented, when they were accessed, and when they were printed. Letting him know that these ideas were protected company property might have stopped him right there."

"Well, John, you've painted a picture for when this would have helped us, but what about if the records don't help us? I'm the company attorney, so I have to consider that as well."

"I see your point. You mean what if someone makes a comment that one of our ideas is similar/identical to an existing product function."

"Exactly, in that situation, we could be liable for treble damages if we knowingly infringed on someone else's intellectual property."

"Yes, I understand that this would not be a good thing if it was discovered in litigation, but I think it is manageable with training. Let's face it, these remarks are probably being made publicly to other employees anyway, and I wouldn't be surprised if it is being made via email. So, even without a central repository, it is probably discoverable, but you just don't know where it is going to pop up. With a central repository, and a little training, we'd know that everything is in one place, and it would be much easier to police. Right now you have to worry about what is being stored on a thousand different PCs, disks, and network drives. It's like a snake hiding in the grass; you never know where or when it might bite you. Besides, electronic storage is the future. What's going to look better in court? A complete set of electronic records, with time/date stamps, notarizations, witnessing, and review steps all outlined in a neat format, or a pile of papers and backups from twenty different PCs?"

"Aaah, I get your point."

"Frank, I know maybe you're concerned about getting up to speed with a new system, but we'll train everyone in no time at all. This will make your entire job easier and more productive. And with Bill asking for cuts, you may be able to escape the axe with increased productivity and throughput."

"John, to change the subject for a minute, what about mergers and acquisitions? Can this central repository be used to help us manage that aspect as well? For example, our recent acquisition of Syntactical Labs went smoothly from a legal perspective, but not many people are aware of the actual assets, like the patents, trade secrets, and innovations."

"Certainly, because you'll be able to add new information to the central repository of information, it will be able to be accessed by both existing and new employees with relative ease. As a side benefit, new employees will be able to get up to speed faster by looking at the entire collection of Medacmet Industries' intellectual property. Connections can be made faster, and development time will be decreased."

"Hold on, you mean everyone will have access to all of our intellectual property?"

"It will be up to you. You'll be able to control access for different people in different roles. For example, people in your department will have greater access than a regular employee. You may choose to temporarily restrict new ideas until they have been vetted, or restrict access based on department or geography. Regardless of how you control access, you need to keep a healthy balance between disclosure and protection. Think about it, if you disclose your intellectual property to everyone and everywhere, it is useless. If you completely restrict your intellectual property, so that no one can access it, then it is completely useless. Intellectual property requires a balance between these two extremes, with the understanding that there will inevitably be some loss."

"I understand, of course that makes sense. So continue describing how this works with mergers and acquisitions."

"No problem. We already talked about the increased collaboration and improved productivity, but you'll also improve your accounting and valuation."

"What do you mean by valuation?"

"With a complete accounting of your intellectual property, you'll be able to demonstrate which ideas and subsequently which inventors had the most impact on current products. This will help you to value the intellectual property and ultimately the value of the innovation that is created. People, technologies, and departments will begin to stand out as innovation leaders, and you'll be able to spend more of your time cultivating these places for additional IP."

"Cindy mentioned that you are going to be helping to solve one of her current technical challenges. Do you think you might be able to solve one of our intellectual property challenges?"

"Maybe. What are you thinking?"

"Well, it goes back to Twinevil Corp. They have patented some technologies that will impact the defense of our patent portfolio, and it would be helpful if we could get additional patents in a few key areas. Right now this is wide open, but probably not on the radar screens of engineering. If we could secure this area, it would help us to create substantial competitive barriers and possibly open up new product innovations."

"That is exactly what we are looking for. By letting the employee population know this, I'm sure we'd get some very good results. I'm guessing that nobody really knows about this except you, right?"

"Yes, I've talked with Cindy briefly, but she is too concerned with the current product portfolio."

"Well, why don't you explain a little bit more about what you're thinking, and we'll create another challenge to address your needs. I can't promise that we will make it available right away, but we can add it to our list."

"That would be great. I've got a few other areas that I've been thinking about lately. I'll send you an email with a few more challenges."

"Thanks, Frank. Well, I'm going to get back to work. I still have a few more meetings before we get started."

"Who are you meeting with?"

"I'm going to meet with HR and marketing, and I also have a meeting with a group of engineers, including Sam English."

Frank chuckled, "Good luck with Sam. He's a fine inventor—one of our best—but not the easiest to work with. He's one of the few who actually understands the intellectual property aspect of what we do. He has over 15 patents."

"Thanks for the heads up."

John and Frank spent a few more minutes fine-tuning Frank's challenge. John explained the finer points of constructing a challenge, including making it specific enough and easy enough to understand for all to participate. John also talked about the rewards aspect, and Frank was more than willing to contribute the company's private box seats to the next three football games. He also pledged to commit several hours to review the ideas and make sure that everyone that participates gets feedback. The challenge list was now:

Ideas for increasing the speed by which the Kidney Dialysis, KD1999, can perform dialysis.

Twinevil Corp currently has a patent for improving performance in dialysis machines by increasing the speed of the motor's RPM in the spin chamber. They have also patented the use of high-performance plastic rotors to reduce the cost, and very specific rotor blade designs that also improve performance. We need to find ways to avoid infringing on these patents, but at the same time achieve the same benefits.

How to Win With Fear, Uncertainty, and Doubt

There seem to be two different kinds of internal IP counsel. The first kind is progressive, understands the corporate value of IP, and the risks of sharing IP with partners and even competitors—we don't need to discuss that kind here. The other kind is more challenging. Like the first, they take their job seriously, and will vigorously defend their organization against all attacks, perceived or real, when it pertains to IP. I can remember one instance when the IP attorney interrupted a meeting with a potential client stating that there was no way that he'd allow the collection and sharing of such sensitive competitive/intellectual information. His argument was they'd be opening themselves up to massive uncontrolled dissemination of their valuable IP, decreasing their competitive position, and giving potential litigants the ability to discover all of their IP information easily by simply downloading the database. Everyone's eyes widened as he continued to paint a horrible picture of devastation and job loss. I recalled that he laughed as he explained the fallacy of electronic capture when their current paper-based system was working just fine. He had all of the company's IP on a spreadsheet on his computer, and was able to track it without any problems. We spent the next few minutes sparring.

Could he give me a report of the disposition of the entire portfolio of his company's IP? No.

Could he guarantee that the written records were not discoverable? No.

Did he know if anyone who left the company inadvertently (or intentionally) took IP? No.

Could inventors collaborate? Yes, they shared their invention disclosure document easily. So, then you do keep electronic copies all over your company that could be discovered? Uh, yes. And you have no control over what those documents contain? Uh, yes. So you might discover that one of your inventors wrote that the invention is similar to a product made by your competitor, opening yourself for treble damages? Uh, yes.

So, with this in mind, do you believe that you've stopped the uncontrolled dissemination of your IP? No.

So, if you had all of this information electronically, you could actually prevent disclosure and possible treble damages? Yes.

In some respect, this attorney was doing his job, protecting his company's IP assets, but he was over compensating. By completely restricting the flow of information, he was preventing innovation, and in reality, he wasn't really preventing the loss of any information when it came right down to it. The attorney's job is to advise you of risk, so that you can make an informed decision. If this guy had been my attorney, he would have tried to prevent me from crossing the street by reciting statistics about pedestrians getting killed, the possibility that I would trip and break my leg (and then get run over), and getting robbed just by being outside. The better advice would have been to explain that there is a risk of getting hit by a car, however, by walking in the crosswalk, looking both ways, and waiting for the green light, much of this risk is eliminated.

Unfortunately, we didn't win this contract, but I was vindicated several years later when that attorney left and they re-contacted us. This time we did win.

The 12th Hour Pardon

"John, we have a problem that I was hoping you could help me with," said the VP of Engineering at one of our clients. He had called to say that one of their most experienced and prolific inventors was leaving their company for a competitor. This person had been privy to nearly every technology, invention, and product since inception and would surely be dangerous. The VP had already talked with their Chief IP Counsel, and they were preparing a lawsuit. They needed me to get some information from our database concerning the information that this person had "stolen."

"Stolen?" I asked.

"Surely," The IP Counsel answered, *"he must have."* This engineer had no idea what was about to happen to him.

First a little background. I've been that engineer—the one who had a lawsuit filed against him—because I was supposedly in the same position and knew too much. Unfortunately, the executives at my company weren't able to call MindMatters, and so they filed a lawsuit against me.

They drained my savings account, subpoenaed my friends, prevented me from working, and added a mountain of grey hair to my head. And, they really had no idea if I had taken anything at all (I hadn't, of course). However, that didn't stop them. To make a very long story short, the suit was dropped and all of the charges were dismissed against me. The amount of lost time and resources—on both sides—was completely avoidable. This was the driving force for the creation of MindMatters.

Our systems have been designed specifically to prevent this problem. Lawsuits are expensive for both parties, and releasing competitive information can be disastrous. It didn't take long to determine that the engineer in question had acted completely and totally appropriately. There was no smoking gun. The VP of Engineering was relieved and the IP Counsel told me that I should use that as a selling point for our system. As for the engineer, he never had a clue how close he came to having his life turned upside down. Inside, I smiled a bit.

Group of Engineers

This was the one meeting that John had been dreading. When he asked Cindy Vinatoni, the VP of Engineering to give him a group from engineering to help with reviews, he was hoping that she'd have been a little nicer. Leading the group would be Sam English, the brilliant, but difficult engineer. Sam English had been with the company for nearly 20 years, and had 15 patents and numerous inventions accredited to him. He was versed in intellectual property legalese, and was the company's top inventor. He was frequently called upon in difficult situations, and had a knack for being able to solve perplexing problems. For all that Sam had going for him, he was also extremely easy to dislike. With the implicit backing from higher executives, he was quick to attack ideas that he didn't agree with, particularly ones in which he had no part, and he wielded his extensive vocabulary of legal and engineering terms like a medieval knight with a battle-axe.

The good news is that he would also be meeting with Janice Koerth, another member of the engineering team. Janice had only been with the company for three years, but she had already distinguished herself as a brilliant engineer. With four patents to her credit, she also had a great deal of experience with IP issues, and was widely respected by her peers. Janice was very diplomatic, and probably her best characteristic was her willingness to listen to people. She would always listen carefully, ask questions, and then provide an opinion. She was clearly blessed with verbal as well as analytical capabilities, a rarity in the engineering field. Thankfully, for some reason, Sam respected Janice, offering the hope that she might be able to help during the meeting.

The last member was Jay Boroke. Jay had been with Medacmet Industries for about 10 years and had a reputation for not rocking the boat. Jay was a welcome addition to any project team, and he could always be counted on to get his job done. Jay was not against trying new things, but he wasn't particularly outgoing either. He kept mostly to himself, and would rather do physics problems than talk with someone about the weather. Jay was always busy and detested meetings; however, he could never escape from being invited because of his insight and expertise.

"Good morning, thanks for coming. As Cindy has already told you, we're beginning a new innovation initiative and I wanted to see if I could get your help."

"Hey John, how long do you think this is going to take today? I have a project review coming up," asked Jay.

"Probably no more than an hour, It'll go pretty quick."

"So, we'll end before the hour? Because I have to walk clear across manufacturing to get there. It seems like all I do is go from one meeting to the next."

"Yes, we'll definitely end it by then. Anyway, I'm not sure how much Cindy told you about what we're working on, but basically we're trying to put together a new innovation process to help us with our situation, most importantly to help with building revenue and reducing costs to fend off the Twinevil Corp acquisition."

"Hate to be the fly in the ointment, John, but we've already got one," stated Sam.

"Have one of what, Sam?"

"An innovation program."

"I wasn't aware. Can you tell me more about it, such as, who's responsible for it and how long has it been around?"

"I'm in charge of it. Been here for the past 10 years. It works just fine."

"Oh, okay. Well, can you tell me a little bit about how it works, Sam?"

"Let me draw it for you on the white board. Where are the markers?"

Jay rolled his eyes, "Make it quick, Sam."

With markers in hand, Sam proceeded to describe the current innovation process.

"All new ideas are forwarded to me via email; however sometimes, someone will just catch me in the hallway. I examine the ideas, and ascertain what technology area they best fit into. Sometimes I'll confer with the inventor about their idea, and ask them to do additional research, such as, checking on other technologies, doing a search at the U.S. Patent and Trademark Office, checking LEXUS, or doing a prior art search. Depending on what we get, I'll forward the idea to others who are experts in the technology area and wait for them to analyze the idea. Then we can decide whether to file a provisional or a One-Eleven A."

"How long do you usually wait for them to analyze ideas?"

"It depends. We're all busy, but I'd say probably at least a few weeks. I expect a thorough analysis and detailed write up."

"Okay, thanks. Can you tell me how they analyze an idea? Is there a specific guideline or criteria?"

"I put together a detailed list of criteria that everyone should consider, for example, how much will it cost to implement, how long to design/build, what the ROI is, etcetera. It's about four pages long, and the reviewers are required to answer all of the information. But, really, each idea is different, so the criteria are adjusted appropriately. Besides, that is what the meeting is for," Sam stated pointing to the next block on the whiteboard.

"After we get their feedback, we'll convene a meeting. We usually wait until we have at least a hand full of ideas to review before we meet. At the conference we'll give it either a thumbs up or a thumbs down based on all of the data. I take all of the good ideas back to Cindy and then we decide which ones make the most sense to pursue. If anything looks interesting from an intellectual property perspective, I'll forward it to Frank Caliente and he'll run it through the IP process."

"How do you define 'good'?"

"It's all based on the write up and analysis. We discuss the idea and then vote, yes or no."

"Do you ever get back to the original submitters concerning their ideas? For example, do you let them know that their idea was rejected and why?"

"Sometimes. We're too busy to get back to everyone. If their idea is good, then they'll know it."

"And if it's 'bad', do you give them feedback?"

"No, not really. If their idea isn't implemented, then it was not selected."

"Hey, Sam. Do you think you could give me the write up and analysis for the idea I submitted a few months ago?" asked Jay.

"Why? It was rejected."

"Because I'd like to see it. Why did you reject it?"

"Didn't get a thumbs up, Jay."

"That's kind of funny, because we're implementing it."

"Well, the version of your idea that I saw was incomplete and not very well thought out. It was rejected for lots of reasons. No marketing information, no manufacturing information, no competitive assessment."

"Oh, I get it. You needed me to 'bulk it up and add a few multi-color graphs,'" Jay said as he laughed.

John jumped back in, "Do you have any regular communications regarding your innovation program? For example, do you let everyone know how well you've done it the past year or which ideas were selected and implemented?"

He looked at Jay and sneered, "The people that do well know about it. As for statistics, we don't keep any. I keep it all on a spreadsheet, so we could easily add up the totals. No one really asked."

"How many people participate in your innovation program, Sam?"

'Out of our group of 500 engineers, we probably have a handful—about 40 or 50—who actively participate. The others are just deadbeats. We usually come up with about three or four invention disclosures per year."

"Hah! That's because nobody knows about it, Sam," interjected Jay.

"What do you mean, there's a link on the main Medacmet Industries intranet site for innovation. It goes right to a web page that explains all about our innovation program. I wrote it myself."

"How long ago? Ten years?"

"What's your point. Everyone logs into that site every day. If they don't read it, then that's their fault. You can lead a horse to water, but you can't make him drink."

"Yeah, we have a whole corral dying of thirst, then," Jay muttered.

There was an awkward silence, and then John continued, "Do you have any specific innovation targets, such as number of inventions?"

"Not really. We're looking for quality, not quantity. We're not going to be one of those organizations that just pumps out garbage patents. Our stuff is quality."

"If I asked someone in the organization if they knew what the steps of the innovation process were, would they be able to answer accurately?"

"The engineers who really matter would be able. Listen, John, I haven't got time to baby-sit these people. If they don't have any ideas to submit, it's not my problem."

"Okay. What about the ideas that you decide to implement? Is there a defined budget for new ideas?"

"We decide on a case-by-case basis. Cindy and I discuss the most promising and we can usually come up with the funding if we need to."

"Who implements the ideas?"

"Typically, ideas are turned over to a project team. Most of the implemented ideas are related to current projects, so we just let that team handle the implementation of the idea."

"Do you ever follow up to see if the idea was implemented?"

"No. If the team doesn't want to implement the idea, then that is their prerogative. If the idea is high-level, then sometimes Cindy will ask. Also, if the idea is forwarded to Frank for IP review, then that is a whole different story. Frank meets with the inventors and manages the process with them."

"Does Cindy ever get involved with the individual idea reviews?"

"No, I deal with all of those issues."

"Do you have any rewards or incentives for innovation?"

Sam chuckled, "Yeah, they continue to get their paycheck."

"That's why they keep leaving for Twinevil Corp," interjected Jay.

"What about a bulletin board or something public like that?" continued John.

"No, but if an idea is patented, then the inventor gets a plaque on the Inventor's Wall. They also get a $500 check."

"Yeah, what he didn't tell you is that you get $500 if you're still at the company. And that's after years of legal work. If I charged by the hour for all of the work that's required to get one of those patents, it would work out to about ten cents per hour," blasted Jay.

Sam put the marker back on the board, and turned to Janice, "What do you think? Think that covers the process pretty well?"

"Sure, Sam. John, Sam is awfully busy with lots of different projects around here, so I think what he is saying is that this is the base template that he uses for the innovation process."

"Good point, Janice. There is a lot of variability in the innovation process, so this is just a template."

"I think what Janice is trying diplomatically to say is that we need a lot of improvement," stated Jay.

"Now, Jay," Janice paused.

"Okay, John, let's hear what you have to say, I've got a meeting coming up here soon."

"Fair enough," said John, "let's get started."

"As you know, the situation around here is critical. I don't think it's a secret that there might be layoffs and other cuts. I personally don't want to be part of that process, and I've proposed to the CEO that we might be able to change some of that through a better innovation process."

John next touched on some of the analytical facts of innovation, "Innovative companies experience profit growth 3-5 times greater than non-innovative companies."

Sam interrupted, "Can you define innovative?"

"Sure, in this case, it simply refers to the percentage of revenue that comes from products less than three years old. Anyone care to guess what percentage of revenue comes from products less than three years old for Medacmet Industries?"

"15," stated Sam.

"Zero," added Jay.

"Nice guess, but it is closer to 3%. The worst part is that this number should be closer to 30%, especially for a technology company like ours. Twinevil Corp is always launching a new product, they are considered one of the most innovative in the marketplace, and their stock price proves it."

"It's quality, not quantity John," said Sam.

"Yes, it is, but if by quality you mean we have no new products, then that is the wrong answer. We have to find a way to raise the number of quality ideas."

John continued, "Considering the situation that we're in, it should be no surprise that over 70% of companies view innovation as their number one weapon to counter increased competition. And, nearly 90% of companies view innovation as critical to their business."

"I could go on and on. Innovative products have higher profit margins, faster payback, better ROIs, and help improve employee engagement. One of the main reasons cited for employee disconnect is not being asked one's opinion on important issues at work that affects them. Another is not feeling aligned with your company's goals, which creates a sense of low value to the group. By plugging employees into the innovation equation and employing the correct tools, these major factors virtually disappear. And so the list continues. I think the simple point is that innovation can be a key to not only our survival, but our dominance of Twinevil Corp."

Sam started, "Listen, John, you've been reading too many self-help books. Everyone's looking for the next killer product. You don't just wave your arms, and say 'hocus-pocus' and then it magically appears!"

"Exactly. Innovation is a business process. It's not just about a few engineers brainstorming in a closed door session anymore. While brainstorming can be beneficial, today, innovation has to be a continuous, repeatable process. And just like our accounting system or manufacturing process, it has to be well-defined, implemented throughout the organization, and managed with checks and balances. Everyone has to be trained, and it has to be ubiquitous in our everyday job responsibilities."

"We have a process, and it has worked for ten years," stated Sam.

"I think what John is trying to say is that we can improve upon the process that we currently have," interjected Janice.

"Right, Janice. You have a great innovation process. You're ahead of lots of folks. But to be world-class, we have to step it up a notch. Sam, you have to be our full-time innovation champion. Innovation is not a part-time job anymore."

"We don't have the budget to make this full time."

"Today, we don't, Sam. But we can change that."

"John, how would you improve upon the current process? And what role do you want us to play."

"Good question, Janice. Cindy asked you to meet with me because you three are some of the most respected and brilliant minds we have. You have not only engineering depth, but intellectual property expertise as well. With your help, we can craft a process that will be implemented throughout the organization, with reach to the very top. Bill is very excited about the prospects, and he told me personally that he will participate in the process. Cindy said the same as well. You'll be part of a team that will be accessing every level in the organization."

John continued on with the explanation of the importance to not only the organization, but also to their careers and the impact they could have.

"The process is going to be simple, but powerful. We are going to start with a couple of things that we'll call 'challenges.' Challenges are areas of opportunity within the organization. They have a very specific scope and time frame. They will be the basic building blocks for our innovation program. Typically, when you create a challenge, you look at the most pressing issues in the organization. This might be the top needs/issues for your customers, how technology can be leveraged into other markets, or the highest cost areas. I've already talked with Cindy about it and she has suggested:

> Ideas for increasing the speed by which the Kidney Dialysis, KD1999, can perform dialysis.

I told her that we will ask the entire engineering organization for solutions to this problem. Instead of just collecting any kind of idea, we are going to ask for ideas that solve this challenge with the KD1999. Incidentally, Frank Caliente gave me another one related to the intellectual property surrounding this challenge. By letting everyone from the entire organization know about the issue, we'll be opening the challenge to solutions of which we may have never even dreamed. Remember, we have engineers from almost every competitor, from different industries, and different disciplines. We'll be invoking the collective brain power of all of them to solve this."

"Cindy gave you this challenge?"

"Yes, and yes, she already told me that you are working on a solution."

"This seems like a waste. I doubt you'll find anything. Why don't we try and create a new one?"

"I'm not sure, Sam. When I explained the concept of a challenge to her, this is what she suggested. She seemed to feel like it would be a good test."

"Do you have any suggestions to improve the challenge that she suggested?"

"Yes, we're not having issues with costs, we're having trouble with the speed at which it is running. It is running too slowly; and that is why we are still working on it. With this modification that I've suggested, we're basically going to be running at almost the same speed as Twinevil Corp's machine."

"Okay then, let's make that change to the challenge so that it gets to the root of the problem more succinctly."

> Ideas for decreasing the manufacturing cost of the Kidney Dialysis, KD1999. Of principal concern is the speed at which the machine performs dialysis: approximately 25% slower than our closest competitor.

John added, "Now I think Frank Caliente's concern is more apparent. We'll have to modify the challenge to include his remarks as well."

"What did he say?" asked Sam.

"He said that Twinevil Corp has a patent on the motor rotor's speed and design."

"Yeah, I know. That's why we had to come up with a different design to increase speed."

"What did you do?"

"We didn't increase the speed or change the rotors, we increased the pressure to push more fluid through the membranes. The problem is it causes more cell damage, but it goes faster."

"Sam, how much more do you think the speed needs to be improved? And how much is it costing us?"

"We need at least a $25\times$ improvement. That would make it $10\times$ faster than the nearest competitor. As for how much it's costing us, that's hard to estimate. Let's just say that our product is currently the slowest on the market, and the most expensive. You do the math."

"Okay, with those changes, I think it improves the whole challenge. Let's add it now."

> Ideas for decreasing the manufacturing cost of the Kidney Dialysis, KD1999. Of principal concern is the speed at which the machine performs dialysis: approximately 25% slower than our closest competitor. Improvements in either the motor's RPM or the rotor blade design will not work, as those modifications are already patented by competitors.

"You mentioned that you're going to let everyone respond to this challenge? Do you mean just the technical people or everyone?"

"Everyone."

"I think it might be a waste."

"Why so?"

"How much is some accountant going to know about this kind of a problem?"

"Well, it depends. Maybe that accountant used to be an engineer. Maybe that accountant has seen this same problem in a previous position. Maybe that accountant is a better engineer than you."

"Ouch, that hurts!" said Jay.

"Countless research studies have shown that the best ideas typically come from within the organization, in some cases that number has reached 70%. There is a well-known example, from the El Cortez Hotel. This hotel, located in California was approximately fifteen stories tall and opened in 1927. As the hotel grew, there was a need to upgrade or add additional elevators to serve the growing number of guests. To accomplish this, architects decided to add a new elevator shaft by breaking through the existing janitor closets on each floor. Since all of the closets were perfectly aligned on top of each other, it would be a fairly straight-forward project. Everyone was in favor of this design, except for the janitor, who was going to lose his job and his closet. He proposed that instead of breaking out the closets, that they install the elevator on the outside of the building. I'm sure that there were probably a few laughs when he made the suggestion, but in the end, they decided to do it. The outside glass elevator was installed in 1956 and was the first of its kind in the world. The hotel managed an incredible architectural accomplishment, and the janitor kept his job; everyone was happy."

"Just like the song, Hotel California. 'Welcome to the Hotel California, such a lovely place…','" sang Jay.

"Sure, Jay. You sing it just like the Eagles. Anyway, as banal as this might sound today, it took an unlikely combination of engineer and janitor to arrive at the solution. Likewise, it took a pretty down-to-earth architect who was confident enough in his own abilities to consider the suggestion of the janitor. People kill ideas because of their own insecurity."

"Okay, great, so now we're going to have a whole bunch of janitors submitting ideas. How are we going to manage this mess?"

"Well, first of all it won't be a mess. Since we're looking for a very particular solution, most people will self-eliminate themselves if they don't have an idea."

"Will these ideas be anonymous?" queried Jay.

"No, people's names will be associated with their ideas."

"Oooh, I don't know about that. I think we'll get better results if we let people put in their ideas anonymously."

"In this example, I think not. We're not asking people for personal comments, just ideas. We're not asking them to rate people or to make disparaging remarks about a supervisor. For the most part, people like to 'have their name in lights.' If someone does feel that they will be submitting a sensitive idea—and they really believe the idea has merit—then they can get the collaboration of others or a supervisor. In general, if you allow anonymous ideas, you end up with a lot more chaff to sort through, as people are much less political and diplomatic. And let's face it, we don't want a public airing, we're looking for ideas. If people are afraid to submit ideas, then we'll have to look at some of the cultural elements."

In fact, John knew that the notion of anonymous submissions was hotly contested, with advocates for both positions. He knew that they could allow anonymous submissions if necessary, but felt that it would be good to start without.

"One other point about anonymous submissions will be the rewards and peer recognition. Most people like to get credit for their ideas, and this will allow it. When asked, most people would prefer peer and manager recognition, so we can play this issue by ear."

"I agree," stated Sam. "If they don't want to put their name on their idea, then that's their problem. Okay, that's resolved. So, now how do we rank all of these ideas?"

"Good question. We'll design a simple 5 to 10 question survey and analysis form that allows us to rank and measure all of the ideas. The questions will cover key areas such as timing, cost, and return. I think it would be wise to start with the form you've already designed, Sam."

"Yeah, I can get you an electronic copy to get started. I designed it a long time ago, so you may want to make some changes."

John continued, "The results can be sorted and categorized and then placed into portfolios for analysis and selection of the top projects. In fact, this will be your main job in the innovation process. Although it some cases it might be a bit tedious, it will be important for all three of you to analyze and comment on each innovation. I expect that it will probably take you a couple of days to go through all of the responses. Given the number of people, I'd guess that we'll have around 60 ideas to review."

"Two days! I don't have that much time," complained Jay.

"Don't worry, I've asked Cindy and she has agreed to provide the resources that you'll need. Besides, this is going to be a very high-profile project. You'll be in front of not only Cindy, but Bill and other executives. This will look good on your resume, Jay."

"John, as I mentioned, I usually just give each idea the 'smell test.' I usually ask people who are experts in specific areas for their opinions as well," stated Sam.

"Sam, actually you bring up a good point: collaboration. As part of the review process, you'll be able to forward ideas to whomever you want and have them analyze them using the same criteria that you'll be using. That way you'll be able to compare your results versus the results of any expert opinions you've solicited."

"John, I'm in. Sounds good, but I've got to get going to my next meeting."

"Understand, our hour is about up. Let me just add one additional comment. You three were specially selected by Cindy for this initiative. You represent the best and brightest of Medacmet Industries, and as a result you carry a lot of weigh with your peers. The innovation process is as much about the logistical parts as it is about the cultural elements. People are going to start talking about this, and they'll look to you three for direction. If you think this is a good idea, then they will too. If you think this idea sucks, then they will too. It's up to you. Just remember, this innovation initiative represents one of our most promising ways to escape the grasp of Twinevil Corp, and I'm asking each one of you personally for your help. Thanks."

"Thank you, John, for getting us involved. I know that a lot of the engineers have good ideas that they'd love to share with others, and this seems like it will be the perfect catalyst. I think you've done a great job incorporating our existing process, and I think it will be well received. Sam, this will be a great opportunity for you to really get a chance to oversee both the technical as well as legal aspects of innovation. I'm jealous," said Janice.

"Yeah, John. I think this might work. Like Janice said, there are probably a lot more people that could be involved. And it will be nice to tie together innovation and intellectual property management. We have always been the quality innovator, now we can bring more of that to the market. Thanks."

And with that the meeting closed. The meeting had gone fairly well. As expected, Janice was on board, and it seemed that Jay was interested as well. Sam was probably still a bit reticent, but because he respected Janice, and because Cindy was behind this initiative, he would probably give it a try.

Meet Sam, the Royal Pain-in-the...

I've met Sam, the obstreperous engineer, more than a few times in my career. Being an engineer myself, I can speak with more conviction about this "fictional" character. While there are certainly plenty who do not fit into this mentality, there are many that still do. The first memorable 'Sam' that I met came to the meeting with a list of problems with our software, some valid, but most were met with rolling eyes from everyone else in the meeting. The problem was that Sam was one of their most prolific and creative engineers. He was given the most difficult problems to solve, and he did a great job. The problem was that Sam was too dominating in the organization, to the extent that no one else could contribute. So, while Sam was certainly talented, he pushed everyone else down. The less experienced engineers couldn't compete with Sam, and just resigned themselves to not contribute to innovation. Since some of the most powerful innovation comes from participation and sharing (particularly with peers), this organization was shutting off a big part of their creativity. I think of the following visual quiz as a reminder of the power of more than one person working on a problem, where the question is to find the number of 'F's in the quote.

> *FINISHED FILES ARE THE RE-*
> *SULT OF YEARS OF SCIENTIF-*
> *IC STUDY COMBINED WITH THE*
> *EXPERIENCE OF EVERYONE.*

When I show this problem, it's rare for anyone to get the answer right themselves. However, when several people are asked together, they easily get the answer: 6. In general, Sam, wants to be helpful and part of the solution, but just needs to completely understand your goals, how it will help the organization, and what it means to him or her. In some respects, this is all that any of us need to participate. So your goal in innovation is to prevent Sam from being the bottleneck, and instead to add his/her expertise into finding better solutions. Engineers really love this stuff.

VP of Marketing

Tony Hernandez was the VP of Marketing. He was known as an advocate for going after new markets, and was always talking with Engineering to see if he could push new products and ideas through. Tony lamented that new technology at Medacmet Industries was typically a 'push,' meaning that Engineering gave him new ideas to sell, not the other way around. He was troubled with the fact that there was never enough customer input into their decisions, and as a consequence, he had a difficult time growing market share.

"Good afternoon, Tony."

"Good afternoon to you as well, John."

"Listen, John, I forgot to bring in my pots and pans, but I did manage to scare up this push pin. Will this be good enough for your soup," as he chuckled.

"That's a good start, Tony, but I think you'll have to throw in a few paperclips and your stapler to bring out all of the flavors."

Before John could even get started, Tony continued, "I'm so glad you're here. I've been pushing for new ideas around here for years. We've been getting pummeled in the marketplace by Twinevil Corp, and I'm not the least bit surprised that they are looking to acquire us. I talked with their VP of Sales, Bernie Pralene, at the trade show a few months ago, and they've offered me a job. It's starting to sound more intriguing, but I'm so damn committed to this place, I couldn't accept. Besides that, I can't stand Bernie. I don't think he ever stops talking about himself. Anyway, I'm all ears. How can I help you?"

"Thanks, Tony, I appreciate you meeting me today. Let me tell you a little bit about what I have planned. We're going to launch a new innovation program that solicits ideas from the entire organization. The difference is that we're not looking for just any idea, we're going to be looking for ideas related to our KD1999 dialysis machine."

"Oh, that'll be nice. That thing is a disaster. I think the only reason people still buy it is because of its quality. It certainly is the slowest and most expensive one out there. How does the challenge work?"

"Well, a challenge is an area of innovation focus. In this case, we'll be asking people to provide ideas directly related to the KD1999."

"You mean, for example, if you want them to design a new machine?"

"Maybe, but it doesn't have to be that complex. It might just be a small modification."

"I'm not sure I understand this challenge thing yet."

"Okay. Let's take airline travel. I'll give you some examples of challenges for the airline industry."

"Now there's something that could definitely be improved. I hate to fly anymore."

"So let's imagine a couple examples of challenges for the airline industry. There might be three different types of challenges; strategic, tactical, and technical. A strategic challenge would be something that would be more esoteric and far reaching, such as 'What services would you be willing to pay for on a flight?' Tactical challenges would be related to existing logistics and programs, like, 'New snack food suggestions.' Finally, technical challenges would be more in the moment, for example, 'How can we improve the padding in the seats?' For each one of these examples, the scope is a little different. Strategic challenges have a much wider scope than technical challenges, but the downside is that strategic challenges would probably get a lot more crazy ideas than the technical question."

"I get it. So, what kind of challenge will the KD1999 be?"

"Good question, I think it is still evolving. Since this is our first challenge, and it will be used to measure the performance of the innovation program, I believe that we will try to craft it so that it fits close to the tactical challenge. Not too much scope, not too little scope. That way, we're more likely to have a success that is easier to implement in a shorter time frame. As we gain experience and credibility with our program, we'll definitely create other types of challenges as well, when the organization and the culture are ready for it. Today, they want immediate, tangible results."

"Well, your challenge is too technical for me. Hopefully, you can dumb it down a little!"

"Okay, tell me what part you don't understand."

"Listen, I sell the machines, so I can tell you all of the features and benefits, but don't ask me how the darn thing works inside. That's for the engineers."

"What can you tell me about the features and benefits?"

"Well, we really have two customers for this machine: hospitals and medical facilities that buy the machines, and the patients who use them. From the prospective of the medical facilities, the machine is very good. It is extremely reliable, it's built very ruggedly, and if it breaks (which it seldom does), replacement parts are inexpensive and readily available. We service our machines within 4 hours. It doesn't help that our machines are the most expensive. It takes a lot of explanation for customers to understand the value. So, from an ROI aspect, we are good, but it would be nice if we didn't have to work so hard. In this economic climate, it's easy to lose based on price. From a patient perspective, we're not so good. The machine is loud, slow, and it looks hideous. If you have to sit in a room for several hours a week with this thing, it's not such a pleasant experience."

"Are there any good points from the patient's perspective?"

"The machine minimizes trauma to the cells during the dialysis process. This is important for patients because it means they are less drained from dialysis, and require less medication before and after the session."

"That seems like a pretty big benefit. We'll add some of these elements to the challenge, particularly related to the customers."

> Medacmet Industries is looking for ideas for decreasing the manufacturing cost of the Kidney Dialysis, KD1999, machine. Of principal concern is the speed at which the machine performs dialysis: approximately 25% slower than our closest competitor. Improvements in either the motor's RPM or the rotor blade design will not work, as those modifications are already patented by competitors. The KD1999 is the first choice for medical facilities because of its ruggedness and durability. Patients complain of the slow speed, the noise, and the design. Doctors favor the device because our method of performing dialysis results in less injury to the patient.

"That's good, but I think you need to word-smith this a bit. I'm not an engineer, so I still get mixed up from all of the technical mumbo jumbo."

"Agreed, how's this:"

> Medacmet Industries is looking for ideas to improve the customer experience of the Kidney Dialysis machine, model number KD1999. Our customers include not only medical facilities, but also doctors and patients. Medical facilities and patients complain of the machine's slow speed, noise, and poor aesthetics. So we're looking for your help to improve any one (if not all) of these characteristics. You'll get bonus points if your suggestion also lowers the overall cost of the machine, particularly how much it costs to manufacture. We've included links to the machine's technical specifications and marketing materials for further information.

"I like it now. There's a chance that you might get a few ideas from some of our sales and marketing folks," he chuckled.

"That's what we want."

"Now, John, are you going to create more of these challenges?"

"Yes, the goal with the first challenge is to establish the innovation program, and start out with something that everyone can sink their teeth into. After we start this challenge, we'll create new ones every few weeks, with the goal that at any one time, employees will be exposed to between two and four active challenges."

"What do you mean by active?"

"In order to maintain interest, the challenges have a specific time frame for when they are visible, and therefore active for users to submit ideas. After that date, the challenge is archived."

"Does that mean it's gone forever?"

"No, it just removes it from the view of most employees. Administrators and managers will still have access to the challenge. And everyone will still have access to all of the ideas that were submitted. We've seen that by having a specific start and end date, employees are more likely to participate, and by varying the challenges, people are more likely to come back and look again at the new challenges."

"So, I would be able to look at all of the ideas that get submitted?"

"Yes, absolutely. After some time, the list of ideas will become quite extensive, and you'll find that it's a treasure chest of value. So, when you have a customer that's looking for something that we haven't been able to solve, you might very well find the solution among the historical and archived ideas. Plus, you'll find that ideas that were rejected in the past, or that may have been declined for reasons that aren't germane today, and consequently might be ripe for implementation."

"That will be useful. I'll have a window into exactly what Engineering is doing. No more guessing games."

Abruptly, the meeting was interrupted by Katie Croslinski, one of the marketing team members.

"Hey, Tony, can you tell me about the... sorry, I didn't see that you were in a meeting."

"No problem. John, let me introduce you to Katie."

"Nice to meet you, Katie," as they both extended their arms to shake.

"I'll get back to you later, Tony," as she prepared to leave.

"Just a minute. I'm talking with John here about a new innovation program. He's putting together a new innovation process where we are going to focus on finding solutions to customer problems."

"That does sound interesting," Katie remarked, "I talk with physicians that use our products nearly every day. I could certainly give you a few ideas. I'm on the front lines of selling our systems as well as defending us against competitors. It can be brutal at times."

Tony added, "Katie is one of the best and smartest too."

"Now Tony, don't say anything that I can't live up to," she laughed.

"John, maybe Katie can help you with your challenge. Especially since you've added a marketing component to it now?"

Before John could speak, Tony continued, "I'm not kidding about her being smart. The physicians really respect her opinion, plus she has a Ph.D. in biomechanical engineering."

"Okay, I'm leaving before this gets too thick," Katie quickly interjected, "however, if you need help, I'd be more than willing. I like what you're trying to do and it could end up being a huge benefit to our customers. I'll come back later, Tony." And she quickly exited Tony's office.

"What do you think, John."

"I'm intrigued. I'd be lying if I told you that I don't already have my hands full with the engineers that I'm working with, but it would be helpful to have someone from the marketing department part of the review process."

"Alright, it will be up to you. Anyway, where were we? Oh, yes, what about me though, what if I have a challenge?"

"Like what?"

"Well, my sales team is always uncovering some new requirements or customer concern. What if I made one of those into a challenge?"

"Yes, that would be a great idea. You'd be able to create a customer-related challenge and then find a solution to your problem. You'd be able to create market pull, something I know you'd like."

"You bet. Maybe rejecting that job offer wasn't such a bad idea after all."

"Tony, I'll make sure that it wasn't."

After the meeting, John pondered the result. The conversation was fairly typical. It's not uncommon for a disconnect to exist between marketing and engineering. Different personality types are attracted to each of these areas, and they sometimes don't mesh well. If John could create a stronger link between the customer-centered activities of marketing and the technically-centered activities of engineering, it would be the perfect result. Marketing would be feeding specific customer requirements to engineering to find solutions quickly. Katie could be the answer to getting marketing more involved.

Grandma's Attic

"Are you kidding me? Is this all of our stuff?" That was the reaction I got from the VP of marketing at a major manufacturing organization. Sadly, his comments are fairly typical. In most companies, there is a distinct "neutral zone" between engineering and marketing. Engineers point at marketers and exclaim that they, "sell things and technology that we can't create, then get upset when we can't deliver." Conversely, marketers point at the engineers and state that they are never building things that address the customer's needs. In the case of this marketing executive, his comments referred to the list of innovations that engineering had developed, but never moved forward. He viewed this information as a veritable gold mine of new features and functions that he could sell. "If I had known we could do this, I would have been able to sell more," he continued. As it turns out, both groups are operating in a vacuum, and by sharing information, the entire organization will benefit. So how do you do this? The simple way is to build your innovation challenge with market-facing information. My personal opinion is that engineering dislikes the constant interruption of marketing requests, i.e., "change the color to red," then just as quickly "change the color to green," and it begins to become difficult to respond to all of these "rushes" when you could just make one design that would handle all of the requests. On the other hand, marketing is talking directly with customers and gets the full brunt of problems, requests, and issues. It's hard to ignore a feature request when it's your biggest customer, or to not want to make a color change when you know you'll have a huge jump in sales. Because of their direct interaction with the customer, they have a better sense of what works and what doesn't work, and the face-to-face contact is a powerful conduit for innovation. Challenges can be directed towards marketing, "how can we best use technology ABC with our current customers?" or directed towards engineers, "how can we solve this customer problem?"

Director, Human Resources

John was looking forward to his meeting with Mike Orlowski, the director of human resources at Medacmet Industries. Mike was the stereotypical human resources director: he enjoyed the human elements of the work environment, and wanted to make sure that everyone was happy with their role in the company. Mike had been with Medacmet Industries for nearly 30 years, and although he was open to new ideas, he was technology-phobic and communicated mostly through interoffice mail.

"Good morning, Mike."

"Good morning, John."

"Thanks for meeting with me, Mike. I'm not sure if you've heard about what I'm doing with Bill yet."

"No, not yet, but I'm sure you're about to tell me," he laughed.

"You're right about that, Mike. I'm working on an innovation program."

"Sounds interesting. Are you trying to come up with new ideas?"

"Yes, I talked with Bill about how we might be able to help increase our profitability—and possibly fend off Twinevil Corp—by implementing some new innovation business processes."

"We could use that kind of help. Do you want me to give you some ideas?"

"Not exactly, I'm here to talk with you about the people side of innovation. While we have a lot of the process side figured out, the people and cultural side needs more detail. Innovation, particularly asking for people to come up with new ideas, is an optional process. People don't have to do it to keep their job, and if we don't consider the human side, our process is likely to fail."

"I'm glad you stopped by. I've been very interested in this subject for some time. I've read lots of articles on innovation. We've even tried it here a few times."

"Yes, I heard that from Sam English. He told me about his innovation program."

"He has an innovation program? That's news to me."

"Yeah, he told me that he has had an innovation program in place for about 10 years."

"Well, if he has, he never covered any HR aspects."

"I believe that. I don't think he was really concerned with that element."

"Anyway, as I mentioned, not including Sam English, we've tried innovation a few different times at Medacmet Industries."

"Can you tell me more about those attempts?"

"Certainly, and attempts they were. We tried it about 10 years ago for the first time. It was a project that was driven by IT, you know, with the widespread use of the Internet at that time, the IT group came up with a little web program for people to submit ideas. As I remember, the website was pretty nice."

"What happened?"

"Unfortunately, the only people who really knew about it were the folks from IT. The program was invented by a couple of smart engineers, but it was one of those 'spare time' projects. No real resources, no sponsorship. The process was driven by a few committed individuals, but most of the ideas were considered junk. It was also used as a dumping ground for complaints, and it rapidly became more of a place to complain than to innovate. Because of their lack of resources, they ended up not following up with many of the ideas, people quickly lost interest, and it fell into disrepair."

"Sounds typical for many first-time innovation programs. Were there any others?"

"Yes, we tried again about 5 years later. This time they tried to fix the mistakes from the first attempt. It really started as a business development exercise. They were looking for 'big ideas,' the ones where we might make $1 billion in sales. They wanted to make sure that they didn't get a bunch of little ideas, so they purposefully made the scope larger. This time it included sponsorship by senior managers, and as a result it all but eliminated everyone in the organization from participating. The focus was on what they could do with current resources, and they never provided or even considered additional resources. Also, there was so much senior oversight that there was almost zero tolerance for failure. You had to either submit an idea that was going to create $250 million in sales in 3 months, or you might as well forget it. Because it was sponsored by the executives, it was considered to be one of those projects that was part of your job, and so there was no real incentive to participate. They made it part of everyone's performance review, but what ended up happening is that people would basically just submit the project that they were already working on. They got nothing new, just the same old rehashed projects. Like the first, it died after about six months. No one really heard much after the initial launch. The people that did submit ideas never really heard back."

"Did you participate?"

"Minimally. I was asked to come up with a rewards program for the rollout and to create the initial communications for the monthly newsletter."

"How did that work out?"

"Okay at first. I came up with a point-based rewards program. I don't remember the details, but it was something like one point for every submission, 50 points if the idea was accepted, and so on. They got hung up on the points, couldn't come up with what they believed were the perfect awards. I spent two months talking to various reward vendors; it really got out of control. Eventually, they just decided to give out cash. Like the point system, they could never really decide how much money to give out, so that is when they decided to just award for ideas that yielded patents. Inventors received $500 in cash for patents that we received. It really didn't capture the spirit of innovation."

"What about the communications?"

"That went a little better. I put together a few articles for the company newsletter, and drew up some signs for the bulletin boards. We did put that information up, but only for the rollout. The executives quickly lost interest, and it was like pulling teeth to get any more help with communications."

"Yikes, doesn't sound too promising."

"No offense, John, but I'm surprised we're trying it again."

"No offense taken, Mike. I've worked on these programs before, and I think between the two of us, we can put together a much better program."

"What do you have in mind, John?"

"Well, to begin with, we have sponsorship from Bill."

"Be careful with that, John."

"I understand. Bill will not be running the program, but he has agreed to sponsor the communications and make sure that resources are available.

I know that he doesn't have time for the day-to-day work, but I can get him to some of the big stuff like congratulating winners and shaking loose roadblocks."

"The second thing that we'll be doing is targeting specific areas within the organization. Unlike in the past, we're not looking for any idea. We'll be looking for ideas that are specifically related to the KD1999 Kidney Dialysis machine. We call them challenges."

"But won't you dissuade people if you are only looking for one type of idea?"

"Yes and no. If people don't have an idea that is germane to the KD1999, then yes, we don't want them to submit an idea. The goal is to minimize waste. We're going to have people who are particularly interested in solving issues related to the KD1999, and we won't have the time or resources to address every idea—regardless of its merit—for this challenge. The other side of the coin is that while we are looking for ideas for the KD1999, it will only be for a short duration, maybe one or two weeks, and then we'll change the focus. As we get better, we'll have several different challenges for people to respond to at any given time."

"What about communication?"

"Absolutely. I'll be looking for your advice, particularly in this area. We'll of course need initial communications, but I'd like to dedicate a small portion of the monthly newsletter to innovation. The people who have made special contributions, not just submissions, but reviewers also. The communications will be ongoing. I will also ask for your help in modifying the challenges so that they will appeal to a broad audience. In fact, I have the challenge right here:"

Medacmet Industries is looking for ideas to improve the customer experience of the Kidney Dialysis machine, model number KD1999. Our customers include not only medical facilities, but also doctors and patients. Medical facilities and patients complain of the machine's slow speed, noise, and poor aesthetics. So we're looking for your help to improve any one (if not all) of these characteristics. You'll get bonus points if your suggestion also lowers the overall cost of the machine, particularly how much it costs to manufacture. We've included links to the machine's technical specifications and marketing materials for further information.

"Another aspect of this program is that it will be computer-based," stated John.

"I'm not much of a computer guy, John."

"That's okay. I'll help you. However, today, most people interact with computers on a daily basis, so communications will actually be a little bit easier. Everyone reads their email, so we can use the newsletters as well as the computer to keep up with communications."

"That sounds pretty good. What about rewards and recognition? I think the point system I came up with for the second program might be a good start."

"You're absolutely right. Non-cash rewards go much further, so we should be able to have some fun with it."

"I tried to convey that to the execs last time. I told them that tangible rewards that people could be proud of would be best. I like the idea of giving trinkets for initial participation, like a pen or t-shirt, but substantial rewards, such as a cell phone, or television for the real prizes. Also, considering our dismal success during our last two attempts, I think it will be important to reward failure."

"How do you mean?"

"I wholeheartedly believe that we should give out rewards for the best ideas, but what about the ideas that were 'pretty good' but not quite good enough. I'd like those people to be eligible for rewards as well. The reward point system that I developed did just that. You might get 500 points if your idea was selected, but you might also get 100 points if your idea was feasible and viable, but not selected. It keeps everyone in the game."

"There are a couple of other benefits to the computerization of this process, Mike."

"What else do you have up your sleeve?"

"Well, the records that we'll be keeping can help you with performance reviews as well as exit interviews."

"What do you mean?"

"Think how useful it will be to be able to pull up a listing of all of the things that a particular employee has helped to invent, review, comment on, and analyze. If you really want to get a true gauge of someone's contribution to the organization, this will be an excellent mechanism for allowing this to happen."

"You mean I'll be able to see what ideas someone has entered?"

"Yes."

"Isn't that dangerous? I mean, don't we have intellectual property in the database?"

"Yes, we will, but it will be protected. You may not get a detailed description of the exact ideas, particularly if they are in the patenting process, but you'll still get a sense of how much that individual has contributed. This same information will also help you in the exit interview process."

"How?"

"Is it true that when people leave you interview them?"

"Yes, we go through a standard checklist."

"Is there any place on the checklist that discusses intellectual property?"

"Yes, they have to sign saying that they won't use any of our intellectual property. If they refuse to sign, then we withhold their last paycheck and other benefits."

"But do they know what intellectual property you're referring to?"

"Well, I assume that they know. They were working on it."

"Mike, as an engineer, I can tell you that it is sometimes very difficult to know what belongs to you and what belongs to the company. For example, the company is not allowed to prevent someone from using their general skills and knowledge in a new job. You couldn't tell a plumber that he wasn't allowed to be a plumber for anyone else, just because he left your company. He may not be able to use a specialized tool that Medacmet Industries invented, but that would be it."

"That makes sense, John."

"The plumbing example gets more complex when you're talking about integrated technologies, trade secrets, and complicated concepts. The system we use will be able to delineate what is true intellectual property and what isn't. When someone is in their exit interview, you'll be able to give them a listing of all of Medacmet Industries' protected intellectual property and specifically tell them that they are not allowed to use those pieces. It should make the interview go smoother."

"Sounds easy."

"It should be. Sometimes engineers will inadvertently disclose information without even realizing that it was valuable. It protects them and it protects us."

John wasn't sure that Mike was in complete agreement with the intellectual property aspects of this, but he didn't raise any objections. John decided to get back to the human resources elements.

"Getting back to the environment," stated John, "I'd like to get your help with one more part."

"Sure, what is it?"

"This is definitely more in your area of expertise, but I'd like your permission to send out a brief survey to the entire population of Medacmet Industries to assess their level of innovation awareness."

"What's the point? I already confessed that our prior innovation experiences have been pathetic. You have an open invitation to get started."

"I appreciate it, but the survey may uncover unforeseen problems."

"Like what?"

"For example, we'll ask questions to determine whether employees feel that they have adequate time and/or freedom to create and submit ideas."

"Sounds kind of predictable."

"Hopefully, it will be. However, I came across a situation in a previous position where employees were not allowed to submit ideas because they were required to bill 40 hours a week to certain contracts. The problem is that this 'requirement' was not a written requirement, but rather a 'highly desirable' requirement by most managers," John motioned by holding up both hands and quoting with his fingers. "As a result, employees initially did not submit any ideas for fear of reprisal for not billing 40 hours. We uncovered the issue and made a simple change to solve the problem. Even if it is completely predictable, it will give us a baseline in which to compare our before and after results. I'm an engineer, I can't help that I find comfort in numbers," John laughed.

"Sure, I'll help arrange it. Might turn out to be interesting."

"Great, then I can count on you for two things: helping with the communications, including the survey, and with the rewards."

"Sure, I always seem to leave a meeting with more to do," Mike joked.

Human Resources

Early on in my innovation journey, we launched a website for a group of engineers at a large defense contractor. Everything seemed to be in place, including executive commitment. However, we had almost no participation and only a paltry few idea submissions. Back at the drawing board, I talked with several of the participants and discovered that they were committed to working 40 hours per week, and had no time to spare. It turned out that when you are working on government contract work, you get paid for every hour you work, usually with profit as well!). So, if all of your engineers only work 39 hours per week, you start to lose a fairly large sum of money that can't be recovered. Hence, managers absolutely would not allow a single minute to be spent on anything other than billable contract work. The result was no innovation.

"But, hey," one might argue, "they could submit ideas before or after work and during lunch." True, but the problem is that if they submitted a good idea, they would be asked or required to work on it to study its potential. As a result, by submitting an idea, they were basically adding more work to their already busy schedule. Not too many people like to create new work for themselves, particularly when even if the idea was investigated and found to be promising; they wouldn't get to work on it anyway. Totally demotivating. The solution was simple: engineers could add new ideas, and any promising ones would be "funded" by a project budget that would allow them to cover their 40 hours per week. Because this same company was struggling to meet revenue targets, the new innovation was a welcome addition, and was able to turn around their depressed growth rate.

Bean Bag Chairs and Whiteboards

I give a presentation I call WIFM, and it stands for "What's In it For Me?" It's one of the basic tenets of establishing a culture of innovation. Basically, it says that if you don't understand and address the motivating factors for your people, then you're not going to get anywhere.

I've seen some really incredible setups for innovation. In one company, they built (yes, built) a brand new 20,000 sq. ft. building exclusively to foster innovation. It was beautiful inside, and was designed to look like an old town village inside. It was complete with state-of-the-art electronic bulletin boards, bean bag chairs, lots of open space, plants, waterfalls, and every other creativity-inducing thing that you could think of. It looked like it was designed by the Disney Imagineers, however, I think it was more of a projection of the CEO's image of innovation rather than a functional space. They brought in a bunch of high-powered brains, gave them a ton of money, and told them to be innovative. After about two years of lackluster results, they called us. Why? Because they didn't answer the question, "What's In it For Me?" In a professional environment, this might mean career advancement, peer recognition, or freedom to explore. However, it all depends on you finding this out before you start your program.

Sometimes all you have to do is ask.

Information Technology

John thought the meeting with IT should be pretty cut and dry. All he needed them to do was to enable a simple single-sign-on script for the new system. Other than that, they would have no other responsibilities. Besides, the IT group was always so busy, they'd probably be happy to know that they had no real part in rolling this out. John decided to meet with Napolean Taseme, the director of IT in his office.

"Good afternoon, Napolean. We had a meeting today?" he asked inquisitively.

Napolean was on the phone hunched over the computer. "…I just checked with ITAP and the 10 day SLA is not from them. Maybe it comes from the ITSC? If it helps, then you can mention to them that our people could be locked to one single workstation only. Yeah, Okay. Thanks."

"Can I help you?" Napolean asked.

"Yes, we scheduled a meeting for today?"

"What time is it?"

"3 O'clock."

"Right. I thought we were meeting tomorrow."

"I'm pretty sure it was today."

Napolean tapped on this computer keys and looked at the screen more closely.

"Yep, you're right."

"What do you need," asked Napolean.

"Well, we're going to be implementing a new innovation management system in the next few weeks, and I'm going to need a little bit of help from your team."

"Sorry, we have a freeze. I'm not going to be able to get you anything," stated Napolean.

The phone rang, and Napolean answered, "Taseme."

"The header of the script still has a reference to the MG application and an old date. It needs to be updated with all relevant info, like the author, change log, etcetera. Yeah, by tomorrow. Gotta go."

"Sorry. Like I said, I'm the wrong guy. No resources for any new applications."

"This is a little different. Bill has already approved the resources for this project. We're going to be using a third-party software application to manage the process. All we need from your group is a connection to the log-in process. We know that requiring users to remember another user name and password is a significant hurdle to the acceptance of new software, so we want to be able to use their existing Medacmet Industries user name and password."

Napolean grabbed the phone and dialed, "Amelda? Hey, can you come down to my office. Thanks," and just as quickly he hung up.

John continued, "Anyway, since everyone here at Medacmet Industries signs onto their global account when they log-in to their computer, we just wanted to use the same mechanism."

"Hey, Amelda. Can you show John that idea submission site that you created? He wants to start an innovation management program."

"Sure, can you move?" she asked as she motioned at him sitting at his desk.

"Listen, I don't need another program," John said exasperatedly, "We already have an innovation management program."

"Yeah, I heard you, John, but we already have one. Amelda created one from scratch a few years ago. Should be a lot easier. Amelda, do you have that site up yet?"

"What browser are you using, Napolean?" asked Amelda.

"Firefox."

"No wonder. I didn't program it to work with Firefox. Do you have Internet Explorer?"

"Yes, just minimize my programs, it should be on the bottom right."

John interrupted, "Napolean, the new system already works with Firefox. And quite frankly, this new system has quite a few improvements to the process that we'd like to see implemented."

Amelda interjected, "I can't get it to come up on your machine."

"Never mind," added Napolean.

John continued, "I'm sure that you designed a very nice program for the last idea campaign. For this innovation program, we're going to be using a new paradigm that is significantly different than the one you did before."

"How?" asked Amelda inquisitively.

"People will be submitting ideas against a concept we're calling Challenges." Stated John.

"Instead of having people just submit random ideas, they will be submitting ideas to answer a specific problem, in this case, improvements for the KD1999. After they submit their ideas, they will be automatically routed to an appropriate group of experts based on previously established heuristics. Experts along with reviewers will analyze and rank the ideas to determine which ones should be implemented. They'll be able to compare them with other ideas using portfolios and analysis tools. Implemented ideas will be assigned to project teams and managed through to their completion, collecting statistics on costs and benefits along the way. Finally, participants will be able to monitor the progress of their ideas and earn reward points," emphasized John.

"Ours does that too," interjected Amelda.

"It does?"

"Yeah, users login into the site and enter their ideas on our submission form. The ideas are routed to the administrator. The administrator can set the status of the idea and get reports."

"Does your site have challenges, and/or questions that users answer?"

"No, but we could add some text to the website telling them about the challenge."

"Then every time you wanted to change the challenge, you'd have to change the website, right?" queried John.

"Yeah, but that's not hard."

"Do all of the ideas go to the administrator?"

"Yeah, and we can make whoever we want as the administrator."

"So you can't have the ideas be routed automatically to experts or others?"

"Sure, we just have to add their email addresses into the code."

"So, if you want to make any changes, you have to change the code?"

"Yes, we just change the code."

"Is there a list for the administrator to see all of the routed ideas?"

"No, there is no list, but the admin can just save the emails."

"Okay. What about forwarding the ideas so that they can be reviewed by experts?"

"Yes, the admin can just forward the original email."

"But how does the admin keep track of who has received requests to analyze the idea?"

"I'm pretty sure that you can do that in email."

"What about the participants? Can they manage their ideas?"

"No, but they'll know if their idea gets accepted."

"How?"

"The admin usually tells them."

"I see. And all this would work like this if we had 5000 users?"

"5000? We only ever did it for a handful of people."

"When was the last time this was updated?"

"A couple of years ago."

"Considering that all of these features would require you change the programming code, how long would it take to put all of these other features into your program?"

"I'd have to look at the code. I only wrote a part of it," then after a long pause, she said, "The other programmers are gone."

"I'm sure we could get it up and running, John," stated Napolean.

"I thought you didn't have any resources, Napolean."

"I didn't say that we could do it now."

"If you had the resources, how long would it take?"

"Well, we'd create a project, and then meet with the key stakeholders to develop a requirements document. We'd build consensus, and then produce a functional specification, followed by a design document, database design, user interface design, and of course a prototype."

"And this would take how long…"quizzed John.

"Well, once you figure in the documentation, and user sessions, I'd say a couple of man-years."

"Years!?" asked John

"You can't get all of that for free, John."

"Napolean, that's what I've been trying to tell you. It's already done. In fact, the system has lots of other functions that I didn't even mention, like collaboration, searching, peer reviews, crowd sourcing, external portals, and intellectual property management, just to name a few. There is no way that you'd be able to complete all of that."

"We could assign someone to work on it permanently," stated Napolean.

"So after you complete about 30% of the functionality with several man-years of effort, then you'd assign a full-time person to work on it?"

"Yes."

"And how is this better than what we'd pay for the system, considering that it costs much less than that to buy a completed system, and it comes with an entire company that will continue to improve it every year, a permanent person, if you will."

"I didn't say it would be cheaper. I said that we could do it. Wouldn't it be better to use some of our own people, as opposed to hiring outsiders? Let's face it, John. Times are tough, I'd rather pay our own."

"So you think it would be better to build an innovation system in-house, even though we have no expertise in building this kind of application. So, instead of having Amelda work on systems where she has the skill and expertise—on our own business processes—we'd rather her spend the time on something completely unrelated?"

"I guess. Listen, John. We're up to our asses in alligators here, and they want me to cut costs."

"Maybe you need an innovation system."

"I don't need a smart answer, John."

"It's not, Napolean. As I explained earlier, people will be submitting ideas to solve challenges, in this case, the KD1999. People will be trying to come up with ways to improve the machine from a cost, user, and market perspective. There is no reason why we can't come up with a challenge for your group."

"What do you mean?"

"Tell me, Napolean, what is your biggest headache in IT?"

"Easy. We have a whole stable of legacy systems. We have a tough time finding people who even know how to deal with these dinosaurs anymore."

"Okay, then maybe we create a challenge that is directed to the IT department, looking for solutions in this area."

"Everyone in IT already knows this is a problem."

"Yes, but did you ever ask them for their opinions on a solution?"

"They can come to me whenever they want!"

"Yes, I can tell that you're very approachable," John muttered, "Did you know that almost three-fourths of solutions to these kinds of problems are solved by internal people?

"We could create a challenge, direct it to IT, or maybe even to everyone in the organization. You never know who may have solved a problem like this in a previous job. Then, we'd come up with a few cool rewards, like a new computer or some other cube toys, and see what we get. You might be pleasantly surprised. I implemented a system just like this for another IT organization, and they found millions of dollars in savings within the first few months of use."

"Millions?"

"Yes, millions. This is the power of focused innovation."

"Is this system web-based?"

"Yes, it's web-based and has all of the necessary controls in place to protect our data and provide a high level of security for our intellectual property. You can help me with that by getting a simple single sign-on login script to work with the new system."

"Do they use SAML?"

"Uhh, what's that?"

"Security Assertion Markup Language. That is the protocol we use to communicate with external systems. If they use that, then it will take about an hour to setup."

John, Napolean, and Amelda continued discussing how the innovation program would be used to solicit ideas for the KD1999, and how they could participate with that challenge as well as create their own. John confirmed with Napolean later in the day, that indeed SAML was used, so the script was installed and worked out perfectly.

Move Out of the Way, I'll Do it!

A few years ago, my wife ordered new crown molding for our family room. To match our furniture, she picked out a fairly unusual style and design. When the wood was ordered, the salesman just assumed that his carpenter would install it and gave us a price that included installation. "Ha, I laughed. I'll take care of the installation, I can handle it," I said as I waved my hands across the sky in a magical motion as if it would be installed in a flash. The salesman was gracious and mentioned that most of their customers use them for the installation, but that they would be more than happy to deliver it. Now, I've installed crown molding before— in square rooms. But this room had several very odd corners and angles, not to mention that the wood was a complex design. Nonetheless, I setup my equipment on Saturday morning, made a few measurements, checked it twice (because I know the old adage, 'measure twice, cut once'), and I was not about to ruin this wood. So, I cut, and cut, and cut, and refine, and cut, and sand, and cut. I didn't give up easily, but eventually I did. "Gosh," I thought, "this is harder than it looks." Although I expected the labor cost to suddenly increase, it didn't and the original carpenter graciously came back and installed it.

In an effort to cut costs or speed up your effort, you invariably decide to do it yourself. In some cases, it pays off, in others it doesn't. Innovation is plagued by the belief that it can be done easily. Everyone just imagines that they likely to come up with ideas themselves and that all they need to do is collect and review ideas, and then pick the best ones. Simple! The problem is that it is more difficult for some, and takes too long for others. If you're planning a wedding, most people don't plan on baking the cake, and if they did, they'd probably realize that they need to be a master baker. For others, even if they could do it themselves, it would be a waste of time, and that their time would be better spent doing other things, such as building the culture.

Such is the case with IT and idea management systems. It's rare not to find an existing "system" someplace within the organization, but there is usually a reason why it's covered in mothballs—it didn't work right.

Summarizing the Process

Having met with most of the key players in the process, John Jones believed that he had gotten the innovation program off to a good start. Since he had talked with each of the stakeholders individually, John decided that for the next phase, he'd meet with all of the interested players to formulate a rollout plan.

Before he scheduled the meeting, he worked with Mike Orlowski, the HR director on building the survey and getting the results. John knew that even though he had tried to cover all of the bases with the major players, there could still be issues lurking within the culture.

"Mike, I'm glad you could meet with me so quickly on this survey."

"No problem, John. As I told you, I have a keen interest in innovation, not only from a personal perspective, but also for the good and welfare of Medacmet Industries. During my tenure here at Medacmet Industries, I've put together quite a few of these surveys. Although none were related to innovation, I can help you with formulating the questions and getting the surveys distributed and the results collected."

"Great. I have a list of eight areas that I'd like to address as part of the survey. In particular, I'd like to find out the organization's impression of innovation as it relates to the following:

Do we get support for innovating?
How do we innovate?
Are we looking in the right places?
Will we share our ideas?
Do we want to do the follow-through?
Can we get everyone to do it (again)?
Can we afford to do it?
How will we tell everyone?"

"That sounds pretty comprehensive, John. Why don't you explain what you mean by each of these in a little more detail, and I'll work on crafting questions that will get these answers?"

"Sounds like a good plan. Alright, I'll start with the first one: do we get support for innovating? What I'm looking for here is does innovation start at the top of the organization, and filter down through the entire management hierarchy. The basic question we're trying to answer is, 'Is management actively engaged in the innovation process?' As you create questions for this one, I want to know if the participation is with words or actions or both. There's usually always a lot of lip service in support of innovation, but when it comes down to actions, the engagement sometimes wears thin."

"Okay, so I'm going to want to ask questions about management participation, as well as whether managers partake in all the various aspects, like analysis and review."

"Correct. If you think about what metrics we have to measure innovation, that might help your questioning. For example, are there Board of Directors reports and accountability on performance reviews."

"Gotcha."

"The next area: how do we innovate? I want to answer the question of whether the organization believes we have an innovation process currently, and if so whether they know the steps of the process."

"I know what the answer to that one will be," stated Mike.

"You might be surprised, Mike. According to Sam English, he believes it is a well-established process. He just believes people choose to not participate. In any case, you'll get clues to the process by asking whether we have formalized documents that explain the process, and whether people know how to submit an idea if they have one. You might also ask about tools. I know that you mentioned we've tried tools in the past, but I'd be curious if we have anyone else using other things like spreadsheets or shared workspaces. We might find out that there are pockets of innovation within the organization that are fairly well organized. We want to gauge the extent to which this is pervasive throughout the organization."

"Okay, I can make specific references to our old innovation programs as well as documents and standards. Next."

"Are we looking in the right places? This is going to reference whether we have any focused innovation, like the challenges. Once again, it's important that we explain this concept of getting answers to specific questions. Some groups are probably already using this concept without knowing it, others are going to need to understand it. We can get to the root of this by asking about documents and communications in this regard. Most organizations, like ours, have a strategic plan that starts with specific goals for the company and then is filtered down through the organization, so that everyone ends up with a few strategic goals for the organization. We're interested in knowing whether innovation has been strategized in the same way, or if innovation is just totally random."

"So, we're going to be asking questions concerning an employee's understanding of where they should be innovating or creating ideas?"

"Yes, you're pretty good at this."

"I've got a few years experience," he laughed.

"Okay, next is: will we share our ideas? For this, I want to find out the degree of collaboration that is taking place within all of the groups here at Medacmet Industries. Are we using software, such as shared workspaces, email, and project tracking? Is the culture tuned to sharing, or in other words, is sharing promoted and rewarded, or does everyone keep their ideas to themselves?"

"Interesting. I'd say that we don't do such a good job in this area, John."

"That's not surprising."

"A lot has to do with protecting our intellectual property. Frank Caliente usually discourages any kind of collaboration or sharing for fear that we'll lose valuable intellectual property. I'm not sure that you'll change his opinion on that one."

"I've already talked with him about it to some extent. I think he is amenable if we can demonstrate that we have taken the appropriate security measures."

"Okay, so I'll create some questions related to collaboration and sharing among the groups."

"Yes, make sure you tease out whether the sharing is just within a small department or group, or whether it is more widespread. Everyone probably shares with at least one person. I want to find out if it goes beyond departmental borders."

"What about outside the company?"

"Good point. We'll want to know if there is any collaboration with our customers, partners, or suppliers, and to what extent it is happening."

"Anything else on that one?"

"Nope, let's move on to the next one: do we want to do the follow-through? This is a big one. It's mostly related to the review of ideas in the system. For example, will reviewers actually perform reviews, will they actually give feedback and comment on ideas. This is where a lot of innovation management programs fail: reviewers let this slip until it's not being done at all. We're going to want to find out if this is the case with the current innovation program; which I suspect might be part of the issue for the lack of participation."

"Do you really want them to provide feedback on everything?"

"Yes, absolutely. I never said it would be easy, but the results are worth the effort."

"Every time someone submits an idea, they are basically entering into a contract with the entire innovation program. That submitter is implicitly saying that they've put time and effort into their submission, and as a payment they expect it to be reviewed and commented on. Even though a reviewer might not find value in a particular idea, it is seldom the case that the submitter did not. It is disheartening and disrespectful to not review any ideas that are submitted. And truthfully, there could be many reasons why the reviewer might not see value. For example, the idea might be out of their scope of knowledge or there might not be enough details. If you don't respond to that submitter, you're telling them that their idea was not important, and you're discouraging them from ever submitting an idea again. I've seen countless programs fail for this simple reason."

"Sounds like a simple concept, John, but it also seems nearly impossible to go through all of those ideas. How are you going to prevent this from happening this time?"

"Good question. The software that we are using to manage the process helps address this problem in a couple of ways. First, it forwards the ideas automatically to experts within the organization. The system automatically figures out who the experts are and then asks them to rank and comment on the idea. In this way, the review chore is spread out among others. Second, all ideas are visible and 'rankable' by all of the users in the system. Sort of a peer feedback mechanism. This provides another avenue for analysis and further spreads out the reviewers workload. The reviewer can then just look at the organic rankings of not only the experts, but also other reviewers and peers. So, the reviewer can quickly gauge the quality of an idea by looking at the efforts of others. As this process matures, the experts are selected more accurately, and the reviewers are able to gauge the company's interest in an idea very quickly. Of course, the reviewers can also be replaced or the ideas can be rerouted to other departments/groups for more in-depth reviews and analysis."

"Wow. Seems like you have this one covered."

"I believe so. When innovation programs get started, this review process is typically not a problem, but as time moves on, the originators of the project move on, and are replaced by people who may not be as versed in innovation, may not have the interest, or may not have the time. This automated process ensures that continuity of the review process."

"Okay, I think I've got it."

"Great. Next question: can we get everyone to do it (again)? Okay, this one is right up your alley, Mike. I'm referring to rewards and incentives."

"Enough said. You want me to create some questions based on how employees perceive the recognition of their ideas."

"Yep."

"As I mentioned, I put in place a rewards program once before, even though it didn't get implemented. I'm very curious myself to know what sort of perception there is regarding rewards. I know we have something for patents, but I doubt we have anything else. I'm sure that it's no surprise to you, but peer feedback and manager feedback are big pieces of this puzzle."

"You're absolutely right. After all, everyone wants their boss to recognize their contributions. It satisfies both the ego and the pocketbook."

"I'll put together some questions that address both aspects of this. I can tell you that there is nothing on their performance review about this, but some of this may be taking place at lower levels in the organization."

"Next question: can we afford to do it? I want to get at the funding of implemented ideas. How are they funded? From established budgets or is the money 'borrowed' from other projects? Is the funding guaranteed throughout implementation, or can it be pulled for some reason? Funny story. I worked with one organization that would pull the funding from the innovation projects at the slightest hint of any budget problems. The difficulty is that they always had budget problems. As a consequence, getting assigned to an innovation project was a bit of joke. No one really wanted to commit themselves to the project, because the majority of them were cancelled because of funding issues. These innovation projects just ended up being the equivalent of sitting at the beach with a margarita."

"The margarita sounds nice."

"Actually, it was. The funny thing is that it used to annoy the heck out of the people assigned to the project. The reason was that they were typically assigned because they either came up with the idea, or were very interested in seeing it implemented. Getting the funding pulled was a huge slap in the face. They weren't a very innovative organization."

"Yikes. So you want me to build on this theme for these questions?"

"Yes. Consequently, when I talked with Bill about this program, I asked him to commit a certain amount of funding to be used specifically for implementing projects. He wanted to wait until we selected the projects, arguing that he wouldn't know how much to budget until he saw the results. I countered by saying that potential submitters had to know that there would be follow-through on their projects. Who wants to waste their time coming up with ideas that won't be implemented? Not me. Anyway, he saw the point, and agreed to set aside a sizeable amount. We'll definitely want to mention this in our communications with employees about the new innovation program."

"Very nice. I knew you were clever."

"Clever or crazy, I'm not sure which! Okay, last one: how will we tell everyone?"

"Another one right down my alley."

"Yep. I know that you'll do an exemplary job on the communications, but I want to find out if any of this happens at a department level. Do people know which ideas are implemented and what the statistics are?"

"I guessing we're already going to know the answer."

"You're probably right, but we need to get a baseline as well."

"Yeah, I remember, you're a hopelessly analytical engineer."

"That's me."

"Alright, I'll put the questions together and get this out as soon as possible. I'll make sure that I craft a good note, something like this:

> Thank you for participating in this Innovation Survey. We are currently working to gather information about our innovation policies and practices. Your responses will help not only make your organization more productive, but also create a more lucrative environment for you personally and professionally. All of the responses you enter will be anonymous. No identifying information will be collected."

"That sounds perfect. When do you think you'll be able to get this out?"

"Well, it shouldn't take too long. I can probably get this out tomorrow, and have the results back by the end of the week. How's that?"

"Perfect again."

John and Mike continued to discuss the details of the survey, but in general Mike left the meeting very upbeat. It was important to keep Mike involved as his help would be instrumental in maintaining communications.

Einstein's Theory: The Complex Version

The love of complexity in innovation management is an amazing thing to watch unfold. I think that some of it is based on the need to justify the purpose of innovation by making it appear complex; thus teams can justi-

fy their participation and budget. While it is always a continuous process between the innovation team and design, I can think of one example that "takes the cake."

Early in the discussion with a major global banking organization, I was handed their process document that contained nearly 100 pages of descriptions and diagrams. I've looked at some complex processes, but this was definitely over the top. The document described not only a very complex process, with a myriad of steps and conditions, but also radically different steps for relatively similar idea types. After thoroughly under-standing their reasons for the complexity, I suggested that they might be able to simplify some elements of the process in order to make their lives easier as well as make the process understandable to the participants.

With the look of a knowing parent, they metaphorically patted me on the head, shaking their heads, and assured me that each and every step and condition was absolutely necessary. I tried repeatedly throughout our engagement to convince them otherwise, but it didn't work. We dutifully implemented the process, all the while believing that they'd come to their senses when they tested it. Unfortunately, I was wrong. They loved the complexity of the process, and couldn't wait to roll it out. It was like taking a Boeing 747 to cross the street.

They rolled out the system to the entire institution, against my advice, and waited anxiously for new ideas to begin flowing in. Because the group was nearly 10,000 people, they got ideas—lots of them. However, when we looked at the participation rate, it was pathetically low, only in the single digits. Several months went by, and the team tried increasing their communications and rewards, but without much change in participation. Since there were so few ideas to manage and review, the team of nearly a dozen people was reduced significantly until the number of ideas they were managing became "too much." At this point, the team had no choice but to reduce the complexity of the system. When faced with this issue, they began eliminating functionality and simplifying the process. To their surprise, the number of ideas increased, and their participation climbed.

So am I saying that you should have a simple process? Yes and no. It should be obviously simple for the participants, but may need to be more complex for the review and analysis aspects. Innovation is not typically a required process, meaning that participants usually do not have to come up with good ideas to keep their jobs. With this in mind, it becomes a challenge to motivate them to participate, and when you have too much complexity, people just don't bother. I once went to a website to request a 'free' white paper and was presented with a form that contained 15 fields. I passed, because I didn't feel like wasting my time. As Einstein said, "Any fool can make things bigger, more complex, and more violent. It takes a touch of genius—and a lot of courage—to move in the opposite direction."

Survey Results

Several days later, Mike and John meet to go over the results of the innovation survey.

"Well, Mike, what have you got from the survey?"

"Not sure that it's very good, but here goes. According to the results, our management group outwardly encourages innovation, but their actions don't match up with their words. With respect to the process, there are a few departments that are using spreadsheets or other simple capture mechanisms; however there is no one person or entity that is responsible for overall success. We have high-level business objectives, which management believes should be defining innovation, but unfortunately, it doesn't translate into specific actions and innovation areas. Most innovation arises from market maintenance, or in other words, from reacting to customer complaints, and is typically incremental in nature. With respect to collaboration, of course we use typical tools like email and shared folders, and in some cases project management tools; however, most of the use is within departmental boundaries, and we're victims of the proverbial 'the left hand doesn't know what the right hand is doing' cliché. The review of ideas is highly haphazard, and if it occurs, it is infrequent, sporadic, and highly variable. Most submitters report never hearing back on the status of submitted ideas, and there are generally no metrics to track the process. There is a great deal of uncertainty as to what personal incentives exist for innovation. Most employees do not believe that they will benefit directly from innovation. There were some who responded that there is individual recognition; however, it was relatively confined, and was limited to a few departments. Many of the rewards were perceived as trivial or meaningless. And, finally, communication is mostly email or word-of-mouth, and was not consistent or well-defined."

"You certainly said a mouthful."

"The good news is that we have nowhere to go but up," stated Mike.

"You're right about that, but as bad as this is, I'd give us some kudos. You described a very typical organization. While there are many that do better, there are also many that do it worse. Unfortunately, the ones who do it worse, usually don't last in the marketplace for very long."

"So, how do we measure up against others?"

"Well, look at this chart that I prepared."

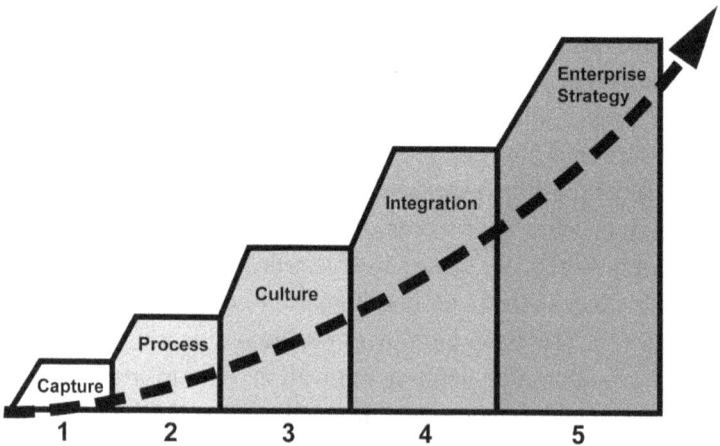

"What it shows is a typical adoption curve for innovation. The lowest level, 'Capture' is that period where an organization's innovation focuses on measuring the number of ideas that they receive. In this area, innovation is typically only successful in small pockets in the organization, and the key is finding these areas and promoting their success throughout other areas of the organization."

"I'm still not quite sure where you're coming from with this chart,"

Mike said inquisitively.

"Okay. Imagine I'm going on a trip from Los Angeles, California, to New York City."

"Alright."

"What are some of the questions that pop into your head about my trip?"

"Such as, 'When are you leaving?'" wondered Mike.

"Yes, what else?"

"Well, I guess I'd be curious to know why, and how you plan on getting there."

"Exactly. If I told you I was going there on vacation, your perception of my trip would be different than if I told you that I was going for business. In the latter case, you might assume that I'm taking a plane, and that I probably won't be doing much sightseeing, whereas if I was going on vacation, I might take my car and do lots of sightseeing."

"If it was business, I would ask you if I could come with you," joked Mike.

"The point is that there would be a natural progression of learning as it related to the trip. Initially, the questions would be general such as whether it was for business or pleasure, but eventually, it would get more detailed, such as specifics about the route and maybe even what I was planning on taking with me."

"Right, so this chart is representing the same type of progression."

"Yes, innovation, like my trip, is a journey. The journey contains many parts, such as the tools, processes, and culture elements to complete the trip. The chart represents the integration of those parts into the entire innovation journey. So, again looking at this chart, 'Capture' represents the first step in the journey."

"That sounds like us," said Mike.

"It's close, but I think we are probably more in the second step, 'Process'."

"Why so?"

"Because the second step is where there are more dedicated resources to innovation, as evidenced by people like Sam English, and to some extent, his boss, Cindy Vinatoni. In this step, the key measure of success is efficiency, and this is where organizations attempt to define and stabilize the process. This again, is Sam. The process is not perfect, but at least he is consistent. With a few tweaks, he'll have a good process. By being able to dedicate more resources to innovation, we should be able to spread the success to other departments. That is my role."

"What about the other levels, do we have a chance of getting to them?"

"Sure. With the implementation of our new innovation program, we're poised to go far. By utilizing our Challenges methodology, we improve participation significantly, and align our business and innovation strategies with appropriate challenges. By completing the survey, we've begun to understand the 'What's In it For Me' issue, and with rewards and recognition programs, for example, even the communications that you'll prepare for the newsletters and such, we'll hopefully break down the WIFM barrier."

- Capture
  ◊ Key measure is # of Ideas
  ◊ Pockets of success
- Process
  ◊ Key measure is efficiency
  ◊ Process is stabilized
  ◊ Dedicated resources
- Culture
  ◊ Key measure is participation
  ◊ WIFM solved
  ◊ Alignment of business and innovation strategies
- Integration
  ◊ Key measure is quality
  ◊ Integration across entire organization
  ◊ Part of daily work
- Enterprise Strategy
  ◊ Key measure is profit
  ◊ Woven into corporate culture
  ◊ Innovation is key asset

"I agree, communications will be key."

"That reminds me, we need to talk about that after we finish this."

"No problem, I already have some ideas."

"Great. Anyway, the software system we install will help us to streamline the process and move us through steps two, three, and four. The software will definitely help integrate the entire organization with its collaboration capabilities, and by installing links to the innovation tools through single sign-on and putting it on our intranet portal links, we'll move innovation more toward a daily activity. The software will support the 'Enterprise Strategy' step by allowing us to keep track of profitability; however, weaving innovation into our corporate culture and treating innovation as a key asset will take longer. For those, our initial programs will have to be repeatedly successful—something that will happen with good challenges—and eventually, its power will be seen at the board level."

"But, John, innovation is supposedly already at the board level."

"I know, that's the funny part. Innovation is usually proposed at a high level without much thought on the logistics required to make it happen. As we figure out the logistics, the results eventually bubble back to the top, and the board realizes that innovation can help support our entire corporate strategy. It's our job to make sure that it 'bubbles.'"

"Roger that. Hey, listen, I need to get going, so we're going to have to discuss the communications later."

"Okay. I'm going to schedule a meeting for everyone involved in the innovation program for tomorrow. Can you just present the plan to the whole group?"

"Sure, but I have to confess that most of it is the brainchild of Nicola Wayne, our communications director."

"No problem. Bring her too."

John sent each person in the innovation program an email scheduling a meeting for the next day. In the email, he reminded them of the importance of the program to the entire company, and the individual tasks to which they had previously agreed. During the meeting, John's plan was to describe the entire process from start to finish, and then fill in the details at that time.

Talk to the Hand

"I've not seen that work before," I said again, this time with more objection in my voice.

"I've done this before," came the all-knowing answer.

Yet, he had never "done it" before. He was at a company where management had rolled out an innovation management system, but he was simply a participant. As we walked one-by-one through the best practices for implementing an effective innovation management program, we encountered change after change. Each seemingly small change took us farther away from the desired outcome.

It had started simply enough. A call from a manager in the R&D department wanting to quickly put together an innovation management program in about two weeks.

"No problem," I thought, "we have a set of best practices that will enable you to quickly put together a winning program." I had done it hundreds of times before, so I knew it was entirely possible.

The basic premise was a push for new products. The VP of R&D had several strategic areas where he saw growth opportunities. He wanted to see what his organization could provide in the way of new ideas. During our initial discussion, we talked about how we should formulate "questions" or challenges that would help direct participant responses toward these areas. He talked in high-level concepts, and as I listened, I translated it into more common language. As I started to suggest some simplified language, he stopped me.

"No," he said. We don't need to dumb it down for this group. These are engineers, and they should be able to figure it out."

"True," I responded, "but why should we make them figure it out? If I asked your engineers what sort of productivity ideas they had, would they know what I was talking about?"

"Probably not—but they should."

I scratched my head because I was trying to figure out why he would want to introduce so much confusion into this process. I can just imagine coming into the office and asking someone if they have any ideas for "NON-SPECIFIC TRANSPORTATION MALFUNCTIONS" versus "my car won't start." It comes across as uppity and it demonstrates a lack of understanding about the audience.

Realizing that I wasn't going to win this argument, I moved on to easier things.

We started talking about timeframe. I suggested no more than 3-5 days for the challenge, and again we had a detailed discussion.

"I want my people to think and give me good ideas," he said. "They need to consider the economic benefits and risks before they make a suggestion."

"Alright, we can still set the limit to just a few days—it spurs people to action," I suggested.

"We don't want off-the-cuff ideas," he replied, "if I give them more time, then I'll get better answers—I've seen this work before."

"How long do you want to give them?"

"60 days for the first part, and 30 more days for the second part."

"Second part?" I asked.

"Yes, during the first 60 days they'll be able to enter ideas, then we'll give them another 30 days to refine them.

"Wow, that's a long time," I remarked. "People really respond much better with a shorter deadline." I gave several examples, but they were dismissed.

We marched on. Next we discussed what sort of information they wanted to collect for the idea submissions. Once again, I suggested simple.

"We want our engineers to look at the competitors, the markets, the risks, and the financial aspects before they submit an idea. I don't want a bunch of ideas that don't meet up with our needs."

"Good," I said, "we definitely don't want junky ideas, but on the other hand, you really can't expect people to write an essay. It's too much work if they don't know that their idea is going to be accepted."

"Well, we're not going to review any ideas that don't contain this basic information."

Like the previous points, I argued vigorously, gave them examples, but to no avail. I was starting to see a pattern, but I pressed on with rewards. I thought for sure that they would seriously consider this.

"OK, how about rewards. In most situations, substantial rewards— not monetary—are offered during the challenge to give an extra incentive to people to submit ideas." I went on to explain that they did not have to be very expensive, they just needed to appeal to the demographics of the participants.

"Definitely. We're definitely going to have rewards," they answered.

"Have you thought about what you are going to offer?" I asked.

"Not yet, but it will be good."

"Great, you need to make the decision and then advertise it before and during your challenge. That way it will have maximum impact."

"Well, we haven't decided yet. I don't think we'll decide until after the challenge is over."

"I'm not sure how much impact an incentive will have after the

challenge," once again offering anecdotes as well as my own personal thoughts on the subject. In my head I pictured a guy selling raffle tickets in the parking lot, "We're selling tickets for $1 for you to win a prize— we're just not sure what the prize is now. But I can assure you that it will be good after we pick the winner!" Yeah, right.

This group launched their challenge pretty much as described and it quickly they began to fail. Noone participated, and the ideas that they did get were tedious, out of scope, and overboard. Luckily, they remembered our discussions and changed many of their initial choices to improve the participation.

Process

"I want to thank everyone for coming today. I know that you're all busy; however, this is critical to our business survival."

"What, no doughnuts?" interjected Sam English.

"They're coming in a few minutes, but only if you behave yourself," John replied with a laugh.

"I asked Nicola Wayne to join us today as well. She has been working with Mike Orlowski and me on the communications plan. We'll get to that later in the meeting. Thanks for attending, Nicola.

"Our agenda today is to go over the innovation process from start to finish. As you'll see in the document that I've given to you, we'll start with the challenges we've created, and walk through the entire process including the capture and submission of ideas to the challenge, the review procedure, analyzing ideas, providing feedback, and idea implementation. Does anyone have any questions before we get started?"

The room was quiet, and John began to wonder how this is going to work out.

Focus

"Okay, well I guess that we're too early for questions. Maybe when the doughnuts get here, that will give everyone some energy. Let's get started with the challenge first. It's on the first page of the packet I gave each of you.

Medacmet Industries is looking for ideas to improve the customer experience of the Kidney Dialysis machine, model number KD1999. Our customers include not only medical facilities, but also doctors and patients. Medical facilities and patients complain of the machine's slow speed, noise, and poor aesthetics. So we're looking for your help to improve any one (if not all) of these characteristics. You'll get bonus points if your suggestion also lowers the overall cost of the machine, particularly how much it costs to manufacture. We've included links to the machine's technical specifications and marketing materials for further information.

Does anyone have any questions with this?" asked John.

"John, I'm wondering if maybe we're answering several questions with this challenge," suggests Janice Koerth, one of the engineers on the review team.

"How do you mean?"

"Well, we could possibly get technical solutions as well as marketing and manufacturing-related ideas. Should we break up the challenge so that we get more segregated ideas?"

"Interesting point. Do you think that submitters will get confused or that reviewers will be confused?"

"Both. From a submitter's perspective, you're asking me for a pretty wide range of ideas: things that cover every functional and market aspect of this device. From a reviewer's perspective, I'm not sure that I personally would be the best person to review potential marketing ideas; it's out of my realm of expertise."

"Alright, I think I understand your viewpoint better. If you were concerned about the review of non-technical ideas, I would have just suggested that you forward those ideas to the appropriate marketing experts for their analysis. Our new system will support finding experts and forwarding. However, because you are also telling me that you believe that submitters will be confused, then I think it will be best to break this into another challenge; maybe more market-related. Then, we can create another review team to look at the marketing-related ideas. How would you suggest that we modify this challenge to better fit the technical aspect?"

"We don't need to break it into another challenge," stated Sam. "I think everyone can understand this just fine. Let's not make this overly complicated."

Nicola Wayne interjected, "Sam, I understand what Janice is saying—it is a little confusing—but maybe we could just give a few examples in the description of the challenge."

"You're the communications expert," he said with a sigh.

"How about this:"

Medacmet Industries is looking for ideas to improve the customer experience of the Kidney Dialysis machine, model number KD1999. Our customers include not only medical facilities, but also doctors and patients. Medical facilities and patients complain of the machine's slow speed, noise, and poor aesthetics. So we're looking for your help to improve any one (if not all) of these characteristics. For example, these ideas could be technical, like new components, parts or designs, or marketing- related, like how to improve the customer interaction, the packaging, or the marketing. You'll get bonus points if your suggestion also lowers the overall cost of the machine, particularly how much it costs to manufacture. We've included links to the machine's technical specifications and marketing materials for further information.

"That sounds like a good improvement," stated John. "Janice, I already talked with Tony Hernandez, the VP of Marketing, and we will be adding some marketing people on the review team. I think you make a good point, and the addition of other experts will serve to balance the review process overall."

"Great, just what we need, a bunch of latte-sipping, bleached-teeth, suit-wearing, know-it-alls!" blasted Sam. "This is beginning to sound more like a pain every minute."

"You should be used to that, Sam" stabbed Jay Boroke.

"Marketing wants to participate, Sam. They are on the front-line when it comes to customer feedback, yet they have no idea what's going on with the technology. I think they could add a new dimension that would benefit everyone," added John.

"That's ridiculous. Customers never know what they want. Before Sony invented the pocket transistor radio, no one knew they wanted one," Sam stated knowingly.

"Good point, but you could argue that Sony's understanding of the overall market combined with the technology was the innovation. Sony didn't invent the transistor or the radio; they combined them and created a new market. Anyway, folks, let's consider the challenge completed. I'll make sure that the marketing people don't have bleached teeth, and we should be fine," said John.

Capture

"Our next item will be capturing the information from each of the ideas. As you can see, I've put together a straw man idea submission form that we can look at. It contains some basic information like the title and the description. I also added a check box asking whether the submitter wants to participate in the implementation if the idea is selected as a project. What other suggestions does everyone have?"

"We need to have some sort of categorization," offered Sam. "I ask inventors to categorize their idea according to key technologies that we use. This helps me to better understand where they are coming from as well as find potential experts."

"That sounds like a good idea. Can you send me your classifications, Sam? We'll add them to the idea submission form. They'll serve a dual purpose: first, as Sam suggests, to help find experts and categorize ideas, and second to easily find duplicates."

"Sure."

"Another thing we should include on our form is the ability for the submitter to identify outside inventors, prior art, technical requirements, materials, testing procedures, and potential competitors," stated Sam. "And, of course, we can't forget to include the user's global ID, home address, and social security number."

"Why don't you just throw in the kitchen sink as well?" laughed Jay.

"This is serious, Jay. Without that kind of information, you can't make an educated decision."

"And just how many people fill those out on your form, Sam?"

"All of them."

"On the first try?"

"Not always. I just send it back to the inventor if it is not completed properly."

"That's probably why so many people participate in your 'idea program,'" as Jay put his fingers up in the air to make invisible quotes.

"It's quality, not quantity, Jay."

"No, it's open innovation, Sam. We're looking for participation across the organization. The challenge aligns the ideas to give us the quality.

We're looking for something novel, not a detailed thesis from one of your cronies."

"Let's put the boxing gloves away, guys. You both have valid points. We want to make sure that we collect enough data to properly analyze and review an idea, but not so much that it becomes burdensome. Sam, some of the information you're looking for is farther down in the process. We can capture that information after ideas are initially vetted. There is no point in collecting the information when the ideas are just concepts."

"What about if we change some of Sam's questions into simple responses? For example, instead of asking for a detailed competitive analysis, we'll just ask the submitter to rate the competitive situation as high, medium, or low," interjected Janice.

"Good idea, Janice," said John.

"Yes, good idea, Janice. We could do the same with all of the fields," stated Sam.

"Janice has a good idea, Sam, but let's keep it simple. The form shouldn't have more than five to ten questions. Any more than that and we'll start losing their attention. However, I do think that some of your other questions should be included—such as some measure of the time and cost—in the same format as suggested by Janice."

"What about related documents?" asked Jay.

"Yes, we'll include the ability to attach electronic documents to the idea. The submitter will be able to browse for files and attachments just like any other application."

"What about collaboration?" asked Janice.

"Sure, we can include other contributors as well. Frank Caliente will love the ability to keep track of all of the potential inventors for an idea."

Sam interrupted, "Good thinking, Janice. Frank and I always struggle with figuring out who all of the people were who contributed to an invention. The ramifications are serious. We lost a patent lawsuit a few years ago to Twinevil Corp because they were able to establish that we inadvertently left out an inventor on one of our patents. Because they could prove that we left off the inventor, the Patent Court ruled the patent invalid, and Twinevil Corp was able to create a competing product."

"You mean not putting a person on the patent can cause it to be invalid?" asked Jay.

Sam continued, "Yep. During the legal discovery process, we had to show Twinevil Corp the records for the invention, which in this case included the notebooks for a couple of former employees. The notebooks clearly spell out their contribution to the invention, but because we didn't know about it, they were left off. Hence, we lost the patent. It was a careless, but costly mistake."

"Okay, I think we covered the IP aspects. Let me ask another question of all of you," asked John.

"What will the metrics be that get measured for each idea?"

"You mean, like Return on Investment?" asked Janice.

"Yes. ROI is definitely something we'll measure, but what metrics do you think Frank Caliente, Cindy Vinatoni, or Tony Hernandez will be interested in after we evaluate and/or implement each idea?"

"That's easy," stated Sam, "Sales."

"Okay, that's a tough one, because sales can sometimes take a long time to generate, especially when we are looking at idea concepts. How about short-term benefits?"

"Well, something related to sales would be a measure of which ideas can be attributed to products that we produce, just like we do when we label our products with patent numbers," stated Sam.

"What I'm looking for is a group of fields that we can use to collect the results and benefits of each idea that is implemented. So, what I'm hearing is that we can associate each implemented idea with a product or product line."

"Correct."

"That's good. Then when we get the total sales for a given product, we can spread it across all of the ideas that contributed to it. That will be more realistic than total sales."

"We might want to measure what area benefits from for a particular idea," stated Janice.

"Can you give us a couple examples?"

"Sure. For example, maybe the benefit is sales, but it could also be increased customer satisfaction, manufacturing savings, inventory reductions, expense changes, labor costs, material costs, cash flow improvements, processing time, reduced waste, brand loyalty, or intellectual property."

"Hold on there, Janice. Let me write all of this down," scrambled John.

"Maybe we should allow for the selection of the benefits that Janice is suggesting as well as an optional numerical representation, just in case they know that number as well." Suggested Jay.

"Wait a minute," interrupted Sam, "I thought we didn't want a bunch of fields on this form?"

"Good point, Sam. This information will be for ideas that are implemented. These fields will not be part of the original submission. They will appear if the idea is made into a project."

"So, this will only be seen by reviewers?"

"Yes, that is the thought. We will probably include others as well, such as the original submitter, and the people involved with the implementation. Does that make sense?"

"Yes, I just wanted to make sure that we didn't over-complicate things," said Sam.

"Good. The last group of fields that I want to collect will be for the purposes of project implementation tracking."

"That'll be easy," stated Jay. "We have a standard project form that includes the project manager, team members, start date, complete date, project number, estimated and actual hours, estimated and   actual budget, and project name."

"Okay, I'll record that information for inclusion on the form. And just like the benefit information, this information will be restricted to reviewers, project team members, and possibly the inventors."

Analysis

"Now that we have the submission part of the equation completed, let's move on to the analysis and review part. Okay, so now that the idea form has been filled out and the user pressed the submit button, the system is going to be configured to automatically find experts and route the idea to those individuals for their opinions. At that same time, the idea will become viewable by all of the people participating in the innovation program, and will appear in the initial review committee: the one for which you folks will be in charge."

"John, tell me more about this 'experts' aspect. How is this supposed to work?" asked Jay.

"Well, it is going to use heuristics, which is a fancy way of saying that it will be using a set of rules to figure out the strength of the connection between the idea and each user's area of expertise."

"What kind of rules?"

"Does anyone here have a Facebook account?"

"Yeah, I do," stated Janice.

"Me too," added Sam.

"Whoaa, aren't you a little old for Facebook, Sam?"

"I have one as well," added Mike Orlowski.

"You need to get with it, Jay. Everybody has one," stated Sam.

"Yeah, right."

"He's not kidding, Jay. I think there are nearly one billion users", added Janice.

"Did you say one billion?"

"Yep. It's not just for your teenagers anymore," added Janice.

"I've connected with many old friends and acquaintances over the last several years as a result. It is a great way to collaborate and share information with others," added Sam.

"I'm glad that everyone has heard of it. Our new innovation program will share some of the same functions as Facebook. Getting back to the experts, if you remember from Facebook, the system will suggest new friends for you based on your interests as well as previous connections and friends. Our innovation program will do the same thing. It will look at a person's interests, expertise, along with submissions and other information to make educated guesses about who would be the best qualified to analyze ideas."

"So, after it is forwarded to these experts, it will also go to each of you in the review committee. From there, you'll be able to see what the experts are saying. If you're satisfied with their recommendations and comments, then you can make your decision on the idea, or you can opt to send it to others for even more analysis. At the same time, you'll be able to see the comments and ratings of the general population of users. So, you'll have several sources of information from which to make your decision. What we need to decide on is what sort of criteria we will use to make that decision."

"John, I don't see why we need to go through this process. I think we all know that the decision is going to come from the gut. You'll know a good idea when you see it," stated Jay.

"I beg to differ, Jay. I've found that some of the most innovative organizations say that trying to make a decision on your gut is one of the biggest mistakes they made."

"Maybe they weren't very smart, John"

"Maybe so, but history is riddled with ideas that were thrown out by their originators as not very good, only to be picked up by others who saw the value. Did you know that most entrepreneurs, who left their companies to start their own business, end up starting a business that their original organization rejected? The number is around seventy percent. And most of those entrepreneurs tried desperately to get those ideas implemented before they left. Even some of the most recognizable inventions, such as 3M's Post-It Notes, were originally rejected before they met with success."

"I'm sure I could give you an example of something that was decided by 'gut feel' that was equally a great success. There are always statistics to prove whatever point you want."

"You're right, I'm sure that there is an example, but the fact that a 'broken clock is right twice a day' is the same principle. Research and common sense prove the point that ideas are way too complex to be considered in their entirety by one person's gut. That's part of the reason for including the comments and ratings of all of the employees. That is also the point of coming up with a standard set of questions for analysis."

"Seems like a lot of waste."

"The standard analysis will also do a couple of other things."

"Like what?"

"Well, for one, it will demonstrate to all of the participants that their idea is actually going to be measured against a standard set of criteria, as opposed to someone's 'gut.' No offense, Jay, but I don't want to subject my hard work to someone's whim. With the analysis questions, you'll essentially be telling each person with your actions that their idea was considered equally with all of the others'. This will help rule out bias, and convince all of the participants that there will be minimal favoritism and politics."

"Yes, but then that means we'll have to analyze each idea."

"Yes, you will."

"I'm too busy for that."

"It's an important part of the process. That's where forwarding it automatically to experts will help you. It will make your job easier."

"If I seem to remember, you've had ideas rejected as well. Did you consider the process fair?"

"No, but that was a different situation," hollered Jay.

"Maybe yes, maybe no. Because it was rejected, you considered the process unfair. As a result, you have less faith in the process, and don't contribute as much."

"Okay, I give. I'll do the analysis. But, let's make it simple."

"Agreed. The second benefit of these questions will be the measurability that you'll get."

"Measurability?"

"Yes, the ability to measure your process and then make improvements. If we use the same criteria for every idea, then we can start to get a sense of what a good idea rates and what a poor idea rates, and program the innovation process to begin automatically weeding out innovations based on those criteria as well."

"It's sort of like Statistical Process Control and Six Sigma wrapped together," stated Sam.

"Exactly. And by using this tool, you'll be able to not only improve your process, but also increase participation in the innovation process. Two birds with one stone."

"So after we analyze these ideas, what will the goal be?" asked Janice.

"Good question. If you look at page 3 in the packet I gave you, you'll see the review process that we're going to follow. In general, it looks like this:

You'll analyze the ideas once and make a general decision about whether you can implement the idea immediately; if you can, then it becomes a project. If you don't have enough information or it is a duplicate idea, then you can either hold it for more information or reject it. If the idea is feasible, but would have a major organizational impact, then it is moved to the next level of review. At this phase, if the idea is judged to have merit even though it will require organizational change, then it is implemented. If not, then it can either be held for more information or declined. If the idea is still feasible, but requires a significant budget, then it is passed to the final review level, where the consideration of significant organization change, as well as significant budgets, are required to implement the idea."

"I'm not sure that I understand this completely. Are we going to have to do three different reviews?" asked Sam.

"This model implies that, yes."

"Too complicated."

"Okay, how about if we simplify this process and just have two steps?"

"How so?"

"Well, you can think of these tiered review levels as different scopes."

"What do you mean by scopes?"

"The first level of review is the easiest scope. In this case, the ideas are 'no-brainers' requiring little if any resources or budget. They will add value to the organization, and will not cause any disruption in normal everyday processes or culture. They can be implemented immediately, and won't require any management approval. An example would be an idea to save paper that requires only that we change the setting on the printer to print in duplex mode. This idea would cut paper usage in half and only requires a minor change to the printer settings.

"The second level is for ideas that are also considered feasible, but would have more significant organization and/or budget impact. If the impact is limited to primarily organizational impact, then a manager would need to make the decision to approve, but because it still requires little or no budget, the decision only needs to consider the cultural or process impact, a scope within a manager's control. For the example of saving paper, if, before you printed, you had to manually go to the printer and flip a switch to print duplex, then this would have an organization impact that may or may not be accepted.

"The last level is for feasible ideas that would have major impact, and are more global in their impact: either impacting the entire organization or requiring a significant budget. These ideas require a decision by top executives and the investment of significant project resources. In the print example, imagine if this required purchasing all new printers for the entire organization."

"Alright, I get it, but I still think this is an overkill for us."

"You're correct, the last stage of review will be completed by Bill and his direct reports. Since we are limiting the ideas by the use of a challenge, we'll have only a very few ideas that will make it to this stage."

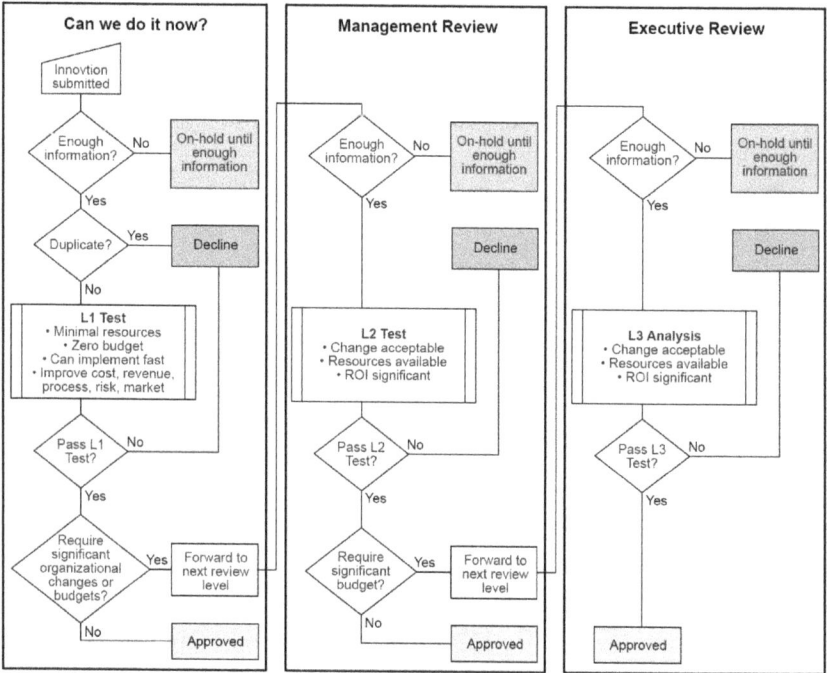

Suddenly the door burst open, "Sorry I'm late. Did I miss anything?" inquired Napolean Taseme, the IT director.

User Access

"Welcome, Napolean."

Sam looked at his watch, "Right on time, Napolean. Let me guess, you're on Zulu-time." Everyone chuckled.

"Sorry, I lost track of time."

"Now I know why you IT guys like to have couches in your office," added Jay.

"Napolean, we've been going through all of the various configuration issues for the innovation program. We were just finishing up the analysis and review section. We're on page 3."

Napolean whipped the document open to page 3 and stared for a few seconds.

"Yeah, this is good. Is this from the workflow engine, John?"

"Yes, we've programmed it to set up a series of tiers for our analysis."

"Yeah, this is good."

"What, you're the expert now?" asked Sam.

"No, but my team built one of the idea submission programs a few years back. Maybe you remember? I was telling John earlier about it. This new system is really nice. It does workflows, single sign-on, and has a complete database. Very nice."

"Napolean, we were just wrapping up this section, maybe now would be a good time to get an update from you on the integration."

"Sure. Integration won't be a problem. We'll login and connect users automatically into the system using our SAML interface."

"How about an explanation for the rest of us, Napolean. We don't live in the wacky World of Warcraft," snapped Jay.

"Simple. Everyone already logs in on their desktop, usually first thing in the morning. So, once you are logged in, in essence the network knows who you are and that you are a valid user. When you click on the link to start the new innovation system, we'll pass over your login information, for example, your name and email, and tell the system that you're good to go. The system will then just automatically log you in. This means you won't have a separate account and password to get into the innovation system."

"What if we don't have an account on the new system?" asked Janice.

"If you don't have an account, then the innovation system will take that same login information and automatically create one for you. Simple."

"That's great work, Napolean," interjected John. "Since a lot of people will be using the system, having an easy sign-on process is critical."

Suddenly there was a beeping sound.

"Damn," muttered Napolean, "gotta go. I'll read the rest of your documentation, John, and get back with you if I have any questions. From my perspective, we're ready to go." And he bolted out the door.

"Who was that masked man?" laughed Jay.

"Wow, we usually don't get that kind of response from IT," added Sam. "What did you give him to make him so excited?"

"A new technology toy. It's a significant improvement over what he built several years ago, and he was impressed at the level of configuration that was possible. Plus, he knew a lot of the shortcomings of the old system, and appreciated the fact that they were eliminated."

"Well, that's one less thing we have to worry about. But, I thought his group was swamped with work?" asked Jay.

"It is, but I showed him how the challenges work, and he was anxious to try it out on some of his own IT issues."

"IT?"

"Sure, we can use the challenge model for a variety of different topics and issues. Napolean wants to try to save time and costs in his department. I talked with Frank Caliente in Intellectual Property, and he wants to use it for developing new patent strategies. There's something for everyone. Now, let's move on to communications. Nicola, do you want to let us know what you've got."

Communications

"Sure. Based on my discussions with you, John, and Mike Orlowski, I've come up with the following plan. First, you mentioned that it was going to be important to demonstrate executive commitment. To address this, I've put this program on the agenda for tomorrow's All Hands meeting. Bill, the CEO, will be addressing this topic specifically. As planned, he'll talk about the importance of the program, his commitment to it, the budget that he has secured, and the participation in the review process. We're going to videotape the event, and make an abridged version available on the company intranet portal, via podcast. You'll also be able to use this information as part of desk-drops as well, but I'll get to that in a minute. Continuing with executive commitments, I've met with each of the vice presidents regarding their role in the process, and have asked each of them to conduct their own lunchtime version of the rollout. I've asked them to reiterate Bill's message, demonstrate how the system will impact their own jobs and responsibilities, and explain how the system will be rolled out, including training. Immediately after the lunchtime meetings, there will be training sessions for all front-line staff. The training will consist of a brief message from their immediate supervisor, a detailed discussion of the challenge model, and a quick overview of how to submit an idea into the system. They'll also be directed to a training website, which will include additional help documents along with the podcast. Immediately after the training, a brief and easy survey will be given to each employee asking them to reiterate what they learned. It won't be difficult; it is designed to get them fired up. If they complete the survey, then they'll get a free t-shirt promoting our innovation program. We've also designed some posters and other graphics that will be placed in strategic places around the organization, such as the cafeteria, entrances, and common areas promoting the program. On the day of the rollout, each employee will receive a desk-drop that contains additional help information, such as a quick, one-page help sheet, as well as guidelines for submitting ideas, and some examples of what information a good idea would contain. The prizes that Cindy has selected will also be highlighted as well, along with the duration of the contest, how they'll win, and when they can expect feedback. Finally, we will continue to place information in our company newsletters, along with information on selected winners. This will be an ongoing effort."

"Wow, Nicola, you've really put a lot into this," stated John.

"I tried."

"No offense, Nicola, but it sounds a little bit like an overkill. You're expecting us to attend, let's see, one, two, three, four meetings?" Jay asked agitatedly.

"Well, Jay. The All Hands meeting will be covering other topics as well, so this is just a small part, maybe 5 minutes. Everyone is always required to attend those meetings unless they have other pressing matters. The second meeting, with your VP—Cindy, isn't it?—is supposed to be brief, maybe ten minutes, and will include lunch. I guess if you want to skip a free lunch, you can, but one of the biggest complaints the communications department gets—concerning all types of rollouts—is the lack of information and education we give the employees. Everyone complains that they don't want to attend meetings, but then they complain when they don't have enough information. The third meeting will be right after Cindy's and will be to train employees on how to use the system, from logging in, to submitting an idea, how the process works, and the potential rewards. It is slated to last about 30 minutes. The fourth meeting, if it can be called that, will be a brief five question survey, and if you complete it, you'll get a free shirt. The survey is completely obvious and is really just to get everyone engaged with the process."

"Yeah, exactly. Four meetings," quipped Jay.

"I don't think you can really call it four meetings," as Nicola held up her fingers to visually quote the 'four.'

"I'm not sure about how you count numbers, Nicola, but all of those numbers add up to four for me. One, plus one, plus one, plus one equals four," as he ticked off the numbers on his fingers.

"Nice, Jay, can you add higher than ten, because you'll run out of fingers if you go higher?" she shot back.

"Jay, the last three meetings will take no longer than an hour, and really, they're all the same meeting. First, Cindy will give you her reasons why this program is important, then you'll be trained, and then get your free shirt."

"What does the shirt look like?"

"We have golf shirts with our mascot, Albert Einstein."

"Cute."

"Yes, they are."

"I also forgot to mention, Bill would like all of you to participate in the All Hands meeting. He feels that it's important to let everyone know the people who will be associated with the process."

"Great," moaned Sam.

"So make sure you wear something nice," as she stared at Sam.

"Don't worry, I'll wear something that won't embarrass you," quipped Sam.

I also talked with Frank Caliente, the IP attorney, and he asked that something related to intellectual property be added to the website. He feels that we should remind everybody of the potential value, and therefore, the proprietary nature of the ideas that we get. I wrote up a couple of paragraphs."

"Thanks, Nicola, I'll take it and add it to the site," added John.

"Well, if no one has any further comments or questions, I think we're adjourned."

What'd He Say?

"I have quarterly meetings where I go over all of the latest results, as well as highlight our strategy and goals for the next few months," stated the obviously proud CEO, *"I travel out to our different divisions and talk with all of our employees. I think we are very connected with what's happening. I think you'll find that our employees know what our strategy is and what is most important."*

In my experience, I'd venture to say that communications, particularly between the executive suite and the workforce, are the most underestimated issue in organizations today. I've never met an executive who doesn't feel that they're a good communicator. Many believe that informal talks, memos, and meetings are adequately conveying their needs and strategies; but most are not. When I talk with the workforce, I invariably hear:

"I have no idea what our strategy is."

"We have a quarterly newsletter, but it only contains birthdays, and summary information that is posted on our external website."

"I go to the meetings, but it never makes any sense to me—I don't know what a 5% margin is, and I have no idea whether that's any good or not."

"Every time someone brings up a difficult question in one of the meetings, it's always saved for later, and is rarely followed up on."

"I have no sense of how I'm doing."

And both sides are guilty. Many employees feel that they've voiced their concerns about under performing processes, new ideas, or new markets. However, when I talk with the executives, I hear:

"Nobody ever told me that (insert your favorite machine, program) wasn't working—I thought everyone liked it."

"At our last meeting, I specifically asked for suggestions, and only received a few unrelated ideas for improving our lunchroom."

So, what's the problem? Two major points: understanding the important issues, and timing. Neither side truly understands the issues that stress the other out. On the employee side, the hot issues may be overtime, cumbersome processes, and poor working conditions. On the management side, it may be slipping profits and competitive issues. At some level, these issues are related—our profits are slipping because we're paying too much overtime—but the problem is usually a lack of understanding and communication. For the employee, receiving time and a half overtime pay hardly seems like it would be affecting profitability, especially when there is no concrete understanding between their wage and the company's costs. Similarly, listening to an executive talk about how 'we need to cut costs', means little to the individual, other than a possible layoff or pay cut. From management's perspective, they have little understanding of what's driving the overtime, possibly assuming that it can't be avoided. Because of this miscommunication, both sides take the path of least resistance. Employees look for new jobs, management tries to reduce labor costs, and neither wins. Unfortunately, this is a true story.

So, how do you fix some of these problems? Simple—just communicate. In our example of overtime pay, the CEO ended up meeting directly with shop floor workers. He explained how overtime pay affects profitability in terms that everyone could understand, and showed how a small change affects the company. With this understanding, employees realized that although they would be trading temporarily higher overtime wages for smaller paychecks, it would result in pay raises later in the year along with potential bonuses and better working conditions. The flood of actionable ideas on how to eliminate overtime resulted in significant profitability improvements.

At Home

It had been a long week, and as John drove home he pondered the official rollout that was scheduled to begin tomorrow. He knew that he had the CEO and most of the executive team on board. They'd always been tuned into innovation, and a key element would be making sure that they continue to participate with their actions; hopefully the All Hands meeting tomorrow would go a long way toward that goal. A big part of that would be the funding that Bill, the CEO, had guaranteed for implementing promising solutions. That was a huge commitment, and would convince a lot of the doubters. Besides, Bill hired him specifically to boost their internal innovation capabilities.

He continued to ponder all of the reasons for failure, and made a mental checklist as he wove through rush-hour traffic. He identified two categories: items he had control over, and those which he did not. In the control list, he had: focus, communications, collaboration across the organization, timed-duration challenges, and non-cash rewards. On the non-controlled list, he had: lack of tolerance for failure, unknown participation, and the 'spare time project' phenomenon. He felt a little better.

He had been able to address the focus issue by creating a top-notch challenge. Everyone on the innovation team seemed to agree that it met all of the criteria for success: appropriate target level, compelling story, appropriate scope, discussion of rewards and the review process. He knew that this was a bread and butter product, so everyone in the organization was bound to know at least a little about it. Coupled with general knowledge of the health care industry—most everyone had a doctor or hospital visit at some point in their lives—led him to conclude that this would not be an issue.

He pulled into the driveway and walked into the house.

"I'm home?!" to which he was greeted with silence.

"Anybody home?"

"Over here, dear. I'm in the kitchen," his wife Clarice answered.

"How was work?" she asked, but before he could answer she began, "you had better talk with your son. He's in the backyard trying to set up some sort of ski jump."

"Good grief. Those skis are brand new."

"You'd better make sure he gets his homework done. He never listens to me."

"JOHNNY, What are you doing?"

"Nothing."

"He is going to kill himself out there," exclaimed Clarice.

"He's fine. He has a helmet on."

"Do you want a glass of wine before dinner?"

"I don't know, I might need something stronger."

"Did you have a bad day at work?"

"No, but we're getting ready to launch that big innovation initiative tomorrow, and there are so many things that could go wrong."

"I thought you told me that you were doing something with the kidney machine."

"The KD1999. Yes, the challenge is all set. That is the least of my worries."

"What's the matter then?"

"Some of the reviewers are a little difficult to deal with."

"Sam?" she asked.

"And others. He is not too tolerant of other ideas, particular ones that he doesn't think are good. The good news is that I have Janice Koerth on the review team as well. She'll be a good buffer to Sam."

"Yes, she is nice. Not like the typical engineer. You're all so difficult to deal with."

"Hey, I resemble that remark," John laughed.

"Sam's no different than you. You're both aiming for perfection. Maybe you should…

"…Will you look at him out there? He's going to kill himself! Go outside and tell him to stop."

"He's fine, he's just out practicing his jumps. Wait a minute. What is Tara doing out there?" as John peered out the window. He jumped out of his seat and opened the door.

"Tara, what are you doing?"

"DAD, Tara is throwing snow at me while I'm trying to go off the jump."

"Tara, leave your brother alone!"

Several more snowballs went whizzing through the air. One nearly hit John in the head.

"TARA, that's enough. Leave your brother alone!" as he closed the door, another snowball hit the door.

"Good grief, what is wrong with your kids?" he asked his wife.

"My kids? They're not mine, they're yours, especially when they're misbehaving. They take after you. I was never that bad."

"Yeah, I know, you were worse!"

"Hey?!"

"It seems like I've been overseeing a circus for the last couple of weeks," stated John.

"Don't worry, John, everything will be fine. Did you run through your checklist?"

"Yes, that's what we've been doing. I finished the last run-through today."

"And, did you get everything finished?"

"Yes, we went through the whole list and checked everything off. There is still always the possibility of a misstep."

"Well, that can always happen, but it never seems to happen. That's why you developed the checklist, isn't it?"

"Yeah."

"I've heard it so often, I even remember some of it. Do you have management buy-in?"

"Yes."

"Do you have the resources?"

"Yes, including all of their personalities and idiosyncrasies."

"Do you have a budget?"

"Yes, Bill has made sure of that."

"Do you have focus, those Challenge things?"

"Yes, that's the KD1999."

"Did you communicate all of this information to the troops?"

"Yes, Nicola put together a world-class communications plan. We have posters everywhere, and training will be synchronized with the roll-out tomorrow."

"Then, I'm not sure what you're fretting about. All of the bases are covered. You'll be fine."

"I know, but there are a few personalities that are a bit resistant."

"Isn't that what the management support is for?"

"Yes, it will be up to Bill to deliver tomorrow. He's a very persuasive speaker, so I'm sure that with his suave manner and Nicola's words, we're going to be in good shape."

Reasons for Failure

- Silo focus
- Minimal sponsorship
- "Spare time" project
- Lack of focus
- Poor follow-up & communications
- Only involved senior leadership
- Focus on "what is available now"
- Lack of tolerance for failure
- Multi-month collection
- Cash rewards were "easiest"

"Besides, John, I think you would agree that everyone's grasping at straws right now with respect to Medacmet Industries. This will give everybody a focus, something that they can embrace that will help them to not only save Medacmet Industries, but also themselves."

"Good point. We've addressed all of the WIFM aspects."

"The what? WIFM?"

"Yeah, the 'What's In it For Me' question," stated John.

"Oh, I get it. Well, it makes sense. Everyone has to understand how they fit into the big picture. Your checklist ensures that."

Several more snowballs hit the windows, but John sighed a breath of relief. It would be an early day tomorrow.

The Rollout

"Hey John, ready for the big day?"

"Absolutely. Are you ready to be creative?"

"We sure are, John. My group's been itching for something like this. It seems like we create, but nobody listens. I'm glad that it looks like that will change."

"It will. Your first chance will be to innovate for the KD1999."

"Yes, I saw that on the bulletin board in the cafeteria. That thing desperately needs something. This could be the big break."

"And you know that the top ideas will be rewarded with an iPad?" asked John.

"Oh, we're quite aware of that John. Everyone wants to win it. I hope you have enough."

"I'm sure we do, but if you don't get it this time, then you'll get a chance for the next challenge, or the ones that follow."

"You mean there will be other innovations?"

"Yes, in addition to the challenge for the KD1999, we'll be introducing a new one about every two to three weeks."

"That's good. We've got plenty of things to work with here at Medacmet Industries, so I'm sure you'll have no problem filling your calendar with things we need to improve."

"I'm sure. Listen, I've got to get going, but thanks for stopping by. I'll see you at the meeting today."

"Yep, I'll be there. Good luck."

John hadn't even gotten through the front door and already he was starting to field questions about the program. So far, so good. As he poured a very large cup of coffee, he heard a voice behind him.

"Make sure you leave room for cream."

"What?"

"If you fill it up all the way to the top, you won't have any room for cream."

"Oh, no problem. I want it filled to the very top. I'm going to need every bit of caffeine I can get today."

"Don't worry. We're all behind you. We've needed an innovation program for a long time. I'm sure that whatever we get will be good."

"Thanks. I just hope we can get everyone to participate."

"I wouldn't sweat it, John. You know that not everyone will participate."

"Yeah, I know, but it would be nice."

"Listen, if management was giving away free money, there'd be some group that would have an issue with it."

John laughed, "Yeah, you're right."

"My group launched a new application last year. We had the same issue."

"What, you had people who complained?"

"Absolutely. We went through a vetting process that lasted almost nine months. Everyone had a say, but in the end, there were still a few who were not satisfied. Most of them ended up participating after a while, but a few didn't. Adversity, It's what makes the world go round."

"I guess."

"The word in the trenches is good. People are ready for this. Make us proud."

"Thanks, I will." He took a huge swig of coffee. Before he got to his office, his cell phone rang. It was Napolean.

"Hello, this is John."

"Napolean here."

"Yes, what's up?"

"I just wanted to let you know that we're completely ready to go. Everything is on our production environment."

"Great."

"Also, I forgot to mention, we were able to import all of the ideas that Sam had collected in his various spreadsheets and loaded them into the system. Now when those people log in, they'll see all of the ideas that they are working on."

"Nice."

"Yeah, I thought so too. Hey, gotta go. Bye."

Before John could even respond, Napolean had hung up. That was some good news. It's always nice to start with some existing data, and Napolean made it happen.

John continued down the hallway to Bill's office. Bill had asked him to stop by this morning to make sure that they were both on the same page. John knocked lightly on the frame of Bill's door as he could see that he was on the phone. Bill motioned for him to enter, and quickly finished his conversation.

"Good morning, John," as he offered for him to sit down.

"Good morning to you as well," John countered.

"Are we all ready to go?" asked Bill.

"Absolutely. As you know, we've laid all of the groundwork. We have the process defined, we've picked our initial challenge, and the training is all prepared. The ball is on the tee, Bill. Just hit it down the fairway and we'll be on our way."

Bill laughed, "Well, I'll try to hit it better than I do when I'm on the course."

"I'm sure you will." John knew that Bill was a scratch player.

John continued, "Bill, your speech this morning will be critical to our success. Many of these programs fail because of the top management's lack of commitment. I really appreciate that you're taking the time to launch this the right way."

"John, I told you at the very beginning that you'd have my full cooperation. Innovation is absolutely critical, period. Likewise, the entire executive team is on board, thanks to you. You've done a remarkable job explaining the process and making everyone feel comfortable not only with the overall program, but how they'll benefit. I think you should be in sales, not engineering," he joked.

"Thank you, Bill. You received the notes that I sent you regarding your speech today?"

"Yes, I did, and I appreciate it. But I can tell you, that personally, I'm so committed to this project, that I really don't need any notes. The future of not only our company, but the entire economic engine is being fueled with innovation. We really don't have any room at Medacmet Industries for anyone who isn't thinking the same thing. But don't worry, John, I won't be telling anyone that they'll be fired if they fail to innovate. I saw your notes about embracing failure."

"Yes, that is an important point. Innovation won't always be successful, but you have to let people know that they can fail, as long as they are trying. We'll keep refining the process to increase the probability of them succeeding."

"Got it. Well, it looks like we had better get going. The meeting starts in a few minutes."

"Good luck," answered John as he left Bill's office. He felt fortunate that he had strong commitment and realized that the exact words that Bill used would matter much less than his visceral belief in the power of innovation. Moments later, John, along with many others, were in the company's largest conference room waiting for Bill to speak. Satellite locations were connected visually.

The All-Hands Meeting

"Good morning," he started.

"Today, in this information age, there are very few things more critical to Medacmet Industries' success than innovation. If we are to succeed in today's competitive marketplace, we need to continuously create and leverage the potential of new technologies, products, and services. As you can see in Chart 1, over the next several years we have challenging growth objectives, and the most effective way to achieve these objectives is through new products that have highly innovative solutions to our customer needs."

Bill continued for about 15 minutes, describing the process in "real time" as it would be deployed throughout the organization. At the end of his discussion, he detailed the next steps.

"Immediately following this meeting, each of you will be attending a brief introduction to the processes and systems that we'll be using to make this all happen. These sessions will describe how innovation will specifically impact each and every one of you, and it will give you the tools to see it happen. As I said when I began, innovation is critical to our company. All I ask is that you make your best effort. Like all of you, I'll be actively participating in the process, and I'll be looking forward to helping innovation drive our success. Thank you."

Conversations of the Engineering Department

Since John was a member of the Engineering group, he was scheduled with Cindy Vinatoni's rollout meeting. He attended to see the reactions. As John's team had laid out in the agenda, each executive was to continue on where Bill left off. Specifically, they were to discuss the challenge, how the process would work, their commitment and participation in the process, and finally adjourn to the actual training.

Cindy's explanation of the challenge was met very positively, as there really wasn't anyone who couldn't see the benefit of improving the KD1999. As she went over the process, she met a little more resistance.

"…and once you submit your idea, it will be reviewed by a team consisting of members from engineering, marketing, and legal. Yes? In the back of the room?"

"Cindy, how does the review process work exactly?"

"Good question. After you submit your idea, it is routed to the aforementioned review team. Each of these members will rank your idea on a variety of aspects, such as cost, timing, and market potential. In addition, ideas will also be automatically routed to people in this room, based on their expertise. So each of you has the opportunity to weigh in on various ideas."

"How do you become an expert?"

"The expertise is determined by your participation in the program, including ideas that you submit, information in your user profile, and analyses that you perform. The more you contribute, the more accurately the system can identify you as an expert."

"Will we be able to see other people's ideas?"

"Yes, each of you will have the ability to search through the entire body of knowledge that we have. This will include not only new ideas, but we've also entered all of the ideas that have been submitted previously. So, if you submitted an idea before, then you'll find it when you log in to the system. Another aspect is that you'll be able to read those ideas, and then rate them—much like you would when you read a news story on the internet—on a scale from one to five. When the review team meets, they'll consider the analyses from experts along with the comments and votes from everyone else, so it behooves you to participate in the process.

"Any other questions? Okay, then you're all adjourned to your respective training sessions. The training is only 30 minutes, and I think you'll find it quite entertaining. Our trainers have worked hard to give you a more 'innovative' experience.

"As you're leaving, I would like to remind you of your part in this process. While this is a completely optional exercise, I hope you'll consider it carefully. I truly believe that innovation is the keystone to our success. This program is designed to bring out the best of that process, and who knows, you might find yourself leading a new project to implement the idea you suggested. Your future is what you make of it. Good luck."

The Review Meeting

Several days after the rollout, and with strong participation, the review team had been gearing up to begin the review process. Because of the wide-spread appeal of the challenge, as well as the endorsement by management, there were a plethora of ideas. John decided to gather the review team together to help them through their review session.

"Good morning, everyone," announced John, "I also wanted to introduce a couple of new people from Marketing that are here today, Chris Highbrooke and Katie Croslinski. Chris is the new business development manager and gets to talk with potential partners and customers about new opportunities, and Katie is our physician coordinator who visits doctors to see how they are using our products and how they suggest we change them. I'm excited that they'll be able to add the customer viewpoint to our discussions and will be help in selecting the best set of ideas. Welcome to both of you. Now, are we all ready to start reviewing ideas?"

"Good grief, John, did you see how many ideas we have to review?"

quipped Sam.

"Yes, I did. You have 57 ideas."

"Looks like we had a lot of pent-up innovation," added Jay.

"I was very impressed," stated Cindy. "We had a lot of interesting suggestions, many of which were feasible. I'm excited to get started."

"I hope it's not this bad every time," stated Sam.

"Bad?! What's bad?" asked Jay.

"Do you really want to have to wade through this many ideas every time we do this?" quipped Sam.

"Well, if it gets us out of the mess we are in, I'd say yes." Added Jay, "Besides, how much time have you spent analyzing these ideas so far?"

"Way more than I should have, I can tell you that!"

"Let's figure it out then. Okay, so you have 57 ideas. How long did you take to analyze each one? A couple of minutes?"

"10 minutes" stated Sam.

"10 minutes! Are you kidding me. There are only 7 questions to answer in order to complete an analysis. You mean to tell me that you spent over a minute on each to answer a simple question?"

"Unlike you, Jay, I'm trying to do a thorough job," stabbed Sam.

"The analysis was designed to be quick, Sam. I may have spent more on some of the ideas, but it didn't take me 10 minutes to do one. Maybe 5 minutes max."

"Well, we'll see who had the best," shot Sam.

"Sure. In any case, you're telling us that you spent 9½ hours on these then? Seeing that 57 multiplied by 10 minutes comes to that amount."

"Yeah, that sounds about right."

"Okay, sure, we'll see who is the closest."

"Boys," interrupted Janice, "let's just start the review so we can see if we have good ideas. I'm not sure that it really matters how much time each of you spent reviewing the ideas."

"Janice's right," added John. "Even if you spent 10 minutes or even 30 minutes on each idea, the real measure is whether we can find implementable ideas. And, in the end, if we end up spending several days to do that, I'd say it would be well worth the time spent. The ROI will definitely be there if we find new product ideas or improvements."

"The other part of this review is that these 57 ideas were also automatically routed to experts for their review, and everyone who participated had the ability to score the ideas on a scale from one to five. So, if we look at the ideas to review, we can see the analysis scores of each of our reviewers here in this room, Sam, Janice, Chris, Katie, and Jay, as well as the scores from several others."

John continued to walk them through the process of sorting the ideas by various attributes, adding comments—even for less than perfect ideas—and letting the submitters know the eventual outcome for their idea.

Toward the end of the review sessions, the review committee members had selected three top innovations:

1. Sonic Vibration. In a typical kidney machine, blood is circulated through a system and waste products are removed. Using existing technology available to Medacmet Industries, called extracorporeal shock wave lithotripsy, which breaks a kidney stone into small pieces, the machine can be redesigned to speed the dialysis process by almost 400%.

2. Transplants. In the ultimate example of market cannibalization, there is a proposal to eliminate dialysis completely by investing in better kidney transplant technologies and methods.

3. Dialysis patients need a blood vessel, or shunt, to connect them to dialysis machines. Because dialysis is done so regularly and is hard on vessels, they are prone to infection and inflammation. The idea is to produce new blood vessels from the patient's own skin, and then use those to replace damaged vessels. This would make it easier and safer to use the machines, and would prevent people from skipping appointments because of the pain and complications.

"So, John, will we award the submitters and co-submitters of these innovations the iPads?" asked Janice.

"Yes, Janice, but we still have a few last steps before this review committee is completed. First, we can see that each of the submitters of these ideas has asked to be part of any project implementation team that might be formed. This is not unusual. We will need to come up with a preliminary project team to take each of these ideas to the next phase: adding accountability to the idea's nurturing and success. Second, we'll promote these ideas to all of the employees, both electronically, and through our pre-established communications program. We'll get Nicola to write articles for the newsletters and other miscellaneous communication points. And last, we need to look at the overall process and make improvements."

"I'm all for that," quipped Sam. "Too many ideas to review," holding up his hands to Jay and adding, "in my opinion."

"Sam, this is definitely something that can and will change. First, let's not forget that this was the first time we did this. Regardless of the challenge, we're going to get more responses. It's just normal. As time goes on, we'll get better ideas to the challenges. We'll also make refinements to the way we construct and advertise the challenges. We can be more specific in our descriptions and restrict the number of participants. However, let's keep in mind that there is a lot of power in tapping the knowledge of the entire company. I'm also going to have to say that your day and a half spent on review was a very, very small price to pay for the magnitude of what these ideas could bring. We can either make these review positions more permanent or perhaps change review members to spread out the tasks. Also, as more information gets added into the system, the system's ability to automatically route ideas to experts will improve, thus making the review process more streamlined."

"I like doing this," interjected Janice.

"I do too," added Katie. "No offense, but I've thoroughly enjoyed reviewing the ideas. As a marketing person, we seldom get to see the things that the engineers are toiling on."

Sam interrupted, "No offense taken, Katie, but some of these technologies are not really marketing-friendly," as he held up his fingers and quoted the word 'friendly' in the air.

"Are you trying to say that we don't understand these technologies, Sam?"

"In a nutshell, yes."

"Well, Sam, I actually have a Ph.D. in biomechanical engineering, and unlike you, decided that I'd rather talk with people about their issues than sit in a lab with my white coat and play with my Bunsen burner. And, I'd venture to say that many of the engineers get very little time in front of the customers, where, in my opinion, the real breakthroughs occur. When you actually watch a surgeon perform an operation, you get a tremendous amount of insight into what works and what doesn't."

"Okay, boys and girls, Let's all behave ourselves."

"Sorry, John. I think we have an ego problem in marketing. We feel like we make an important contribution to innovation, but that it falls on deaf ears in engineering."

"Katie makes a good point. There is a not-so-invisible line between engineering and marketing, yet if you look at our best innovations, even the three we just selected, they are a combination of both. We need to continue to improve this integration; it benefits everyone," stated John.

"Well, I'd like to continue to be a member of the review team, so count me in."

"I'd like to thank everyone for participating in the process. As you all know, there will be more to review. We already have challenge requests from nearly every department, so there'll be no shortage of reviewing. As a next step, I'll take these ideas to the executive committee and continue to foster them along in the process. I'll continue to update the comments and statuses with the appropriate details. Some of you may continue to work on them as well. In the meantime, good job everyone, and I'll see you all next time."

Review Team Principles

During my time with clients, I worked with a lot of review teams. Here are some of the principles and helpful hints that you should be used when creating these teams:

1. ***Commitment****. Obvious, but easily faked or eroded. Make certain that each member not only has the mentality for the commitment, but also put in place safeguards to ensure it. For example, get the idea review team out of the office to a neutral location. I can't tell you how many times someone will pop their head into an idea review meeting, and ask one of the members, "I'm*

sorry, but can I talk to John for just a minute?" Inevitably, the interruption is longer, as John usually must attend to something urgent. It's really hard for me to believe that anyone in the company can't have a few hours without interruption, even the CEO.

2. **Drive**. *Make sure that each member has some interest in pushing at least some of the ideas to completion. Initial ideas are rarely in a final form and usually require help or mentoring to move them forward. Many organizations will create "idea champions" whose sole duty is to move conceptual ideas into implementation, acting as intrapreneurs or expeditors.*

3. **Setup and equipment**. *"Oh, I forgot my laptop," or "I didn't have time to … ." This goes hand in hand with commitment. If they can't remember the tools that they need, or don't have the time to prepare for the meeting, they're doing an injustice not only the review team, but all of the idea submitters. Make it clear what needs to be done beforehand.*

4. **Accountability**. *While it may seem obvious that the idea review team is supposed to "review ideas," the end result may not be so obvious. Will they have the final say or will they have to get their recommendations approved by some other group? If they must get their approved ideas "approved" again, you're taking away some of the respect and prestige of the process. There's no question that some ideas require further deliberation before they can be implemented, but if every one of the ideas must go through an additional step, then you really don't have a review team. Instead, allow the review team to approve ideas within certain parameters such as money, time, or cultural impact. That way, you'll keep the review process intact as well as reducing the need for two teams to review every idea.*

5. **Mix of people and skills**. *If you're reviewing technical ideas, should the entire idea review team be engineers? Likewise, if you're reviewing financial processes, should everyone be an accountant? My answer is no. Your team should contain a*

mix of people and skills that are germane to the types of ideas that you are reviewing. If you're reviewing lots of technical ideas, then it makes sense to have a larger number of technical people. However, a healthy balance of other skills, such as legal, financial, and marketing will provide better results and align with the personality of the organization more clearly. Besides, many people who are accountants today may have been engineers yesterday, in a previous job or organization. It's not unusual to find people with very diverse backgrounds and experience, and in fact you should seek them out. These types can add depth to your team and will often see ideas from a completely different, and sometimes better perspective.

6. ***Permanent members***. *You may also want to consider rotating people on and off the team frequently. While you may give up some of the productivity you'll gain by having a consistent group, by rotating more people, you'll keep the program fresh, and you'll involve more of the organization. For many, this visibility is both an experience and an opportunity to be seen as a contributor, and can provide future benefits for the organization. Additionally, it opens your idea review process up for more people to see how the process works—someone who might feel the process is unfair, would gain an appreciation for the intricacies and difficulties in making decisions.*

7. ***Reward***. *For many organizations, reviewing ideas is just another to-do among an already long list. While many will feel the intrinsic need to be fair and committed, others will lose this feeling quickly. Some rewards can be easy, like recognizing the team periodically, giving them additional titles, and, as mentioned earlier, giving them some accountability and control. However, you may want to consider other rewards, such as team lunches, apparel, or other small tokens.*

Executive Presentation

Several weeks later, each of the ideas had been assigned a project team, and significant progress was being made. John reported on the progress to the CEO.

"Good morning, Bill."

"Good morning, John. Come in."

"Before you get started, I just want to thank you for your hard work on this. I've heard nothing but good things about the entire innovation effort."

"Thank you, Bill. The entire team has worked hard. I was just a cog in the process."

"You're too modest. In any case, tell me what you've got."

"Well, we had almost 63% of all the employees participate in the process. We came up with three solid ideas. One idea uses existing technology —the extracorporeal shock wave—to improve the overall dialysis speed, one idea suggests eliminating dialysis completely be working on kidney issues, and the last idea was to relieve the pain and improve the safety of dialysis by constructing artificial blood vessels."

"The first idea is already progressing quickly. Cindy Vinatoni put together a team that is working to build a prototype. Since we already have lots of the pieces, that idea has the possibility of coming to market rather quickly. Our existing customers are excited about the possibility of this magnitude of improvement.

The third idea is also making significant progress. It turns out that our intellectual property team realized that there is an external team in academia already working on this, and we approached them about licensing the technologies exclusively for our market. They have clinical trials underway, and expect to be able to provide this to patients in the next 18 months.

The second idea is clearly the most ambitious and forward thinking. If we can accomplish this goal, it would change the market radically. However, if we are not part of the research into this, then we'll lose out. Since this is more long-term, we are putting together a consortium of some of the best researchers in this area, making strategic donations to leading research facilities, and participating in the research to be the first to hear about the results."

"Wow. That is impressive, John."

"But, that's not all. Cindy expects to have a new machine to market in 9 months, and our sales group is predicting sales of nearly $50 million during the first 18 months, with even higher projections further out. The market for replacement blood vessels is enormous. We actually formed a new corporation to further this market, and have invested several million for a significant ownership percentage. One of our reviewers and innovation team members has actually just accepted the position of general manager, Katie Croslinski ," concluded John.

"I knew we had a talented group of people, we just needed to tap into it," stated Bill.

"You're right, Bill. Not only have we tapped into it, but we've also enabled a continuous process. This is just the beginning. More challenges are underway, and the results are just as promising."

"What else do we need to continue the success?" asked Bill.

"Well, I'd like to suggest a couple of permanent innovation positions, and the creation of an Innovation Department whose job would be to oversee the entire process. Also, we should establish an investment fund to go after promising equity investments, and have more input into our research consortium. Innovation will radically change how our organization grows and prospers."

Wow, This Stuff Really Works

I was sitting in the office of the VP of a particular division at a large and well-known conglomerate. They were well known for being innovative—very well known. As I sat discussing the value of our solutions, I have to admit that I felt a bit inadequate. While I feel confident in our ability to deliver innovation, on this particular day I was a bit doubtful. They had led the way in innovation in a number of different areas, and I was surprised that they had even given me the time for a meeting. Eventually, they agreed to move forward with our solution, and I set out learning about their organization, adjusting the process, and putting in place our solution. They were attentive, followed all of the steps we recommended, and on the day of the rollout, the entire management team attended to espouse the importance of innovation and asked their workforce to put a serious effort into the journey they were about to begin.

And they did.

Several weeks later, as we reviewed the results, the management team was ecstatic. They had uncovered a number of very innovative ideas and products. Of course, I was pleased as well. It proved that there is always room for improvement—even at the most innovative firms—and accepting that makes them more innovative. However, the most striking part of this whole exercise was the fact that one of the most profitable ideas that they discovered had literally been laying on the shelf for years. Even though this organization encouraged innovation at the highest levels, there were still innovative ideas to be found. By accepting and investigating new concepts, this company continued to be innovative.

It goes to show that the people who are the best continue to be the best, by striving to learn and improve. They simply needed the tools to make it happen.

Epilogue

The CEO of Medacmet Industries, Bill Smith, was able to completely turn the tables on Twinevil Corp as a result of the success of the innovation program. The new markets that Medacmet Industries created caught Twinevil Corp by surprise, and radically changed Medacmet Industries' revenues, margins, and stock price. Although Twinevil Corp was able to sell their stake in Medacmet Industries at a healthy profit, they'll need every penny to fight off Medacmet Industries' advance.

"Do you think you could be convicted of sharing trade secrets with a competitor?" asked Katie.

"I don't think so. Besides, I think I could file a lawsuit because they stole you away from me," laughed Sam, as he and Katie walked hand-in-hand out to the parking lot.

"Who would have ever thought that I'd fall for a guy who wears a pocket protector," giggled Katie, "I guess there's more to innovation than meets the eye!"